A Veteran's Fading Memories

A Veteran's Fading Memories

DANNY HIGGINSON

Copyright © 2016 Danny Higginson

All rights reserved. No part of this publication may be reproduced or transmitted in any form or by any means, electronic or mechanical including photocopying, recording or any information storage or retrieval system, without prior permission in writing from the publishers.

The right of Danny Higginson to be identified as the author of this work has been asserted by him in accordance with the Copyright, Designs and Patents Act 1988

ISBN 978-1-911589-01-3

Published by the Choir Press

BELFAST
October 1972

The warm liquid burst forth spreading around my groin.
Is this the way it's going to end?
The liquid ran down my legs, dripping to the floor.
My bladder had burst. I had pissed myself with fright
I thought I would have been a braver man this this.

Contents

Bradley, The Black Country, 1958 **1**

Army Days **16**

Rsm's Drill Parade **27**

Singapore **32**

The Unit **125**

Belfast, October 1972 **136**

Springfield Road **166**

Notes **176**

Bradley, The Black Country, 1958

The wind was blowing through the wood, rustling the leaves, helping to mask any noise I was making as I was creeping through the scrub and trees, my rifle at the ready, trying not to tread on any twigs which would warn my quarry of my approach. I was sneaking up behind him. I slowly reached out and parted a few leaves on a small bush so I could see him better. He was looking round this big old oak tree with his back to me, his left hand was hanging by his side holding a rifle. I crept nearer and nearer, holding my breath. He was still looking around that old oak tree when I lifted my rifle finger, tightening on the trigger, my rifle was pointing at the back of his head. I was only a couple of feet behind him now.

'Boo' I shouted, and he span, round startled. I squeezed my trigger and my cork hit him straight on the end of his nose. It must have hurt judging from the scream emerging out of his gob. Laughing, I spun around and ran into the woods, looking for another victim.

It was only a small wood in Bradley, a small town in the middle of the Black Country, but it was our wood. All the kids played in it. It beats me how none of us got killed, some of the pranks we got up to.

Running through the wood, I bumped into my best

mate Fred. He was eleven years of age and I'd just turned twelve. We were in different classes in the same school and we got on really well together. I told him I just plugged this kid on the end of his beak and he must have a nose like 'Rudolph'. Our rifles were quite powerful for pop guns.

Laughing, Fred and I made our way home, it was almost tea time anyway. It wasn't easy growing up in the late fifties and sixties. All us kids' families were in the same boat. None of us had much, but we seemed to get by. I can remember once, I had no shoes to go to school in. The cardboard I'd put in my old shoes to cover the holes had long worn out. The holes in my shoes finally got too big to cover with the cardboard, so my dad said I could have his spare shoes to go to school in. So there I was going to school in Dad's shoes – I looked like Coco the fucking Clown, with everyone taking the piss out of me including the teachers. We went to school no matter what.

Truancy was hardly heard of unless you wanted 'six of the best'. Arse hanging out my trousers. Poor, yes, but I never seemed to go hungry. My mum always had food for me. In later life I found out my mum went hungry, sometimes for days, just to feed me. How I wish I could turn back the clock to repay her.

A gang of us playing 'I Spy' in the lit-up window of the shop at the top of our street. It was where all the kids met, in earshot of our mums when they called us in for bed. It was only six in the evening, but they were dark nights. Anyway, we were all playing 'I Spy' and drooling over the sweets in the shop window when I got a tap on the shoulder. On turning, I got this fist full on, right on the end of my snotter. The kid who I had shot earlier in the woods clocked me good style. He turned round and fled with me close up his arse, blood pouring from my nose. I was going to bost him all over the place when I caught him, the little get. He was running towards his house like a whippet, what I wasn't going to do to him when I caught him was no one's business. He beat me to his front door, slamming it shut behind him. Determined to get him, I started banging on the front door, my nose giving me shit. All of a sudden the front door was whipped open and a clenched fist hit me full on my already poor bloodied nose. The door slammed shut once again. The little shit got me again. 'The Bastard.' Crying and holding my nose, blood all over my hands, I turned round and headed for my mum's apron strings.

The little get. But I had to admire his tactics, and I thought, 'Nice one, I'll have to remember that should I ever need it.' Feeling sorry for myself, I thought, 'Fuck playing "I Spy" again.'

*

Billy, another of my mates who lived a few doors up the road from me, his family were the first to get a television in our street. His dad had a good job and could afford one. Some of the kids in our street didn't even know what a television was. Anyway, Mrs Kelly, my mate's mum, used to give all us kids a treat once a week. Every Wednesday after school, she would let us watch kids' programmes on her television from four to five o'clock. Five to four would see at least a dozen kids waiting outside Bill's back door. A couple of minutes before four o'clock, Bill's mum would open the door saying, 'Come on, kids, follow me.' She would herd us all into her living room where Bill and John, his brother, were already sitting on the carpet, in the best speck. Bill's mum would sit us all in rows, looking at this small box on the sideboard. When we were all settled down, she would pass a dish full of sweets round, saying, 'one sweet each, kids.' I never saw a kid take more than one sweet.

After we all got our sweets, Mrs Kelly would switch the television on to the delight of us all. The TV burst into life with a few wiggly lines, then the programme would come on. The first programme I and most of the other kids saw was *The Adventures of Robin Hood*. Seeing the TV burst into life, all the kids clapped and cheered, and then silence as all eyes were glued to the TV. At the end of the programme we all clapped and cheered again. 'Okay kids, that's it for now,' said Mrs Kelly as she started to usher us out again towards the back door. She would stand by the door with a refilled bowl of sweets and she would give every kid another sweet as we filed past her. For the next couple of weeks all the kids were playing with home-made bows and arrows, and every one of us wanted to be Robin Hood or Maid Marion. All of us kids loved Mrs. Kelly.

*

Monday, back in school. I hated Mondays: we had a double maths lesson and I never had a clue, I just could not get my head round maths. I used to sit next to this kid who was good at maths and I used to copy off him. When he made a mistake and crossed it out, I would cross mine out as well.

We always had identical mistakes – that's how the maths teacher caught me out. The book stuck down the back of my pants didn't do anything to stop the pain from 'six of the best'. If anything it made the pain worse. 'Bastard.'

Anyway, after school, I would meet up with Fred and

we would make our way home. We used to take a short cut across a large field then down a small path next to a large scrapyard. The scrapyard was owned by a right old get, he was quite well off and owned a half-dozen scrapyards all over Bradley, Bilston and a couple in Wolverhampton. This scrapyard had large metal railings all around it. The railings were about four inches apart. On the other side of the railings were the two biggest Rottweilers you ever did see. On seeing me and Fred, the dogs used to bound over to the railings, growling and snarling. Fred in his wisdom used to put his face inches from the railings and start pulling faces at them. This sent the dogs into a frenzy, and me and Fred used to have a good laugh at their antics.

We got into the habit of going past the scrapyard every day after school and giving the 'Rotties' a hard time. However, one day, Fred, the idiot, dropped his pants and waved his arse at the dogs just inches from their snarling teeth. This really incensed the dogs. They were going loopy, snapping their jaws inches from Fred's arse. If they could have gotten out they would have ripped us apart. They were going ape shit. So the new thing was on passing the scrapyard for Fred to drop his pants and wave his arse at the dogs, to the great amusement of us both.

It was Friday and the weekend was here, although Fridays to me was one of the worst days in my young life. Fred and me had met up after school and on passing the scrapyard we were surprised not to see the Rottweilers, but we could hear barking. Fred, not to be deterred, dropped his pants again and started waving his arse at the approaching dogs. The dogs, on reaching the metal railings, one of them stuck a long pointed snout through the railings, sinking his teeth right into Fred's arse. The look on Fred's face was total shock followed by the biggest blood-curdling scream I have ever heard. I collapsed to the floor laughing, I just could not control my laughter, my guts were hurting so much that my laughing was painful. Fred went to do a runner and fell over his pants that were round his ankles. He got up and fell down again, all the time screaming. Eventually, pulling up his pants, blood all over his arse, he was away like a rocket. Tears in my eyes, uncontrollable laughter, guts killing me, I could not stand up. I looked across at the dogs, who seemed to have calmed down a little, almost subdued. I don't know what breed of dog they were, but they had long, pointed noses that could get easily between the railings, unlike the Rottweilers. Hence Fred's bitten arse. I could have sworn one of the dogs had a smug look on his face. I still had aching guts from all the laughing, so I started to recite my six times table to take my mind off seeing Fred getting his arse bitten. Eventually, still tittering, I got up and started home. The old get who owned the scrapyard must have seen me and Fred up to our tricks and thought, 'I'm going to get them little shits,' and swopped the Rottweilers for the dogs with the long snouts, maybe from one of his other scrapyards. Passing Fred's house, I saw his dad pottering about in the front garden.

'Where's Fred?' I asked innocently.

'Some bleeding dog has bit his arse,' he said, 'and his mum has taken him to hospital.'

This put me into another fit of laughter. Holding my guts, I ran towards my house with Fred's dad yelling after me and calling me all the little shits under the sun. On arriving home, laughter subsiding, my mum said

'Fred's mum has taken Fred to hospital because some dog's bitten his arse.' My poor aching guts. Here I go again. A triple whammy.

*

Monday morning back in school, it was playtime and lots of kids were playing conkers. The school bully (and every school has one) was doing his rounds. His conker was made of ebony or some other hard wood. His dad was a carpenter and must have made it for him. It looked real enough, but nobody was fooled and all the kids was scared to say anything to him. Anyway, he went round the schoolyard smashing everyone's conkers. After a while he got fed up of this, so he went back to his bullying, just shoving kids around, tripping them up or giving the occasional slap. My mate Fred got tripped up by the bully and fell over, hitting his head and getting a nasty bump. I went over to Fred, who was crying, and said, 'Don't worry, mate, I'm going to get him and he won't be bullying anyone for a while.' Going over to the bully I said 'Hey Jack, fancy a game of conkers?' I knew he wouldn't say no. He just liked beating everyone at everything.

'Yeah, okay, runt,' he said.

He was so confident of smashing my conker he gave me first hit. He held his arm out in front of him, his ebony conker hanging from the string held in his hand. With a smirk on his gob, he said 'Go on, runt, hit it.' I held the string of my conker tight in my right hand, the conker in my left. Here goes, I thought, and I swung my conker as hard as I could, bringing it down with full force and hitting the school bully right on top of his outstretched hand. His eyes bulged as he looked at the instant bump that appeared on his hand – it came up like a duck egg in less than a couple of seconds. Then the scream came as he ran towards the school medical room. The school had a small medical room and a duty nurse. The nurse I'm sure would soon be sending the school bully to hospital because I really walloped him.

The teacher on duty in the playground came across to me and said, 'What happened there?'

I said, 'Sorry, sir, the string slipped out of my hand as I went to hit his conker.'

Satisfied with my explanation, the teacher went on his rounds around the schoolyard.

Fred, holding his head and his arse at the same time, said, 'You must be stark raving mad, he's going to kill you when he gets back from hospital.'

I said, 'Don't worry, Fred, he won't be killing anyone for a few weeks with that hand.' Everyone thought it was an accident, no one in their right mind would do that on purpose. Just after I'd conkered the bully's hand, a few of the kids came over to me smiling, saying, 'Well done, H, the bastard deserved that.'

When me and Fred were alone, I said to him, 'If that bully says anything to me, I will tell him I hit him on purpose, and if I he ever bullies you or me again, I will get him one way or the other and I'm sure he will believe me, well he better believe me for his own sake.' Playtime over, the duty teacher ringing his bell to call us all back to our lessons. My next two lessons would be Art. I said, 'See you at lunchtime, Fred' as I headed back into school.

'Okay, H,' he replied.

I really enjoyed Art, it was my favourite subject and I was quite good at it. Some of my work was hanging on a board outside the headmaster's office. I was proud of that. Lunchtime came and I met Fred in the playground.

Opening our sandwiches, I said, 'What have you got today Fred?'

He looked and said 'Shrimp paste, what have you got?'

I opened up my sandwiches and said, 'I've got dripping. I will swap you one if you want.'

'Okay, H.'

We were over the far side of the schoolyard, I was sitting down on some steps Fred stayed standing as his arse was still giving him grief. We were eating our sandwiches when one of our mates came up to us and said, 'You had better hide, H. Jack's back out of hospital and he's looking for you.'

'Thanks, mate,' I said. 'He won't be able to do much with that hand even if he does find me,' I continued, 'but anyway, thanks for letting me know.'

'Fuck me,' said Fred, 'there's Jack. He looks really pissed off and he's heading this way.'

'Okay, you two fuck off out of the way and I will wait here to see what he has to say.'

Fred and my other mate scampered away before the bully got to me. Jack came over to me. He held his bandaged right hand out in front of him and said, 'You have fucked my fucking hand up, you little shite, and when its better I'm going to fuck you up, I'm really going to hurt you.'

I looked him right in the eye and said, 'No, you're not. Everybody thinks me hitting your hand was an accident, it wasn't. I did it on purpose. If you ever come near me or Fred again, I will do you. I know I can't fight you, but hitting you with a conker was just the start. Leave me and Fred alone or next time it will be a house brick over your head or a cricket bat smashing your knees in.' He looked at me incredulously. I don't think he believed what he was hearing. I said, 'I mean every word I've said to you, just leave me and Fred alone and everything will be alright.' Jack must have believed that I would do what I had said. He never said a word, just nodded, turned round and walked away. I thought 'fuck me, it looks like I got away with that.'

My dad was only a young man at the outbreak of the Second World War when he got called up to join the army like thousands of other young men. During his army training he met a Northern Irishman named Paddy. He and Paddy would become inseparable mates, training and fighting together side by side.

After completing their training, Paddy and Dad joined the South Staffordshire Regiment and then the Glider Battalion. More soldiers got killed when the Gliders landed than was shot by the enemy, so I've been told. Dad survived the landings along with Paddy and later both of them joined the Parachute Regiment. They served together through Normandy, Italy, Germany, France and Norway. They must have seen some terrible carnage, but the only story Dad ever told me of the war was about his best mate Paddy:

It would soon be the end of the war and this could be one of their last paradrops. They had survived four and a half years of blood and butchery. Anyway, my dad told me one night when he'd had a few beers about his last parachute drop. All the parachutists were all lined up in their aircraft. Aircraft door open and approaching their drop zone. Paddy was fifth in line and my dad sixth when the para sergeant shouted 'jump'. Out they went, one after the other, until it came to Paddy's turn. Paddy put his hands either side of the door and froze. He would not jump. Dad knew Paddy was no coward, so he wondered why he wouldn't jump. 'Push him out,' the para sergeant yelled at my dad, 'or we'll miss the drop zone.' Dad pushed Paddy out and jumped out after him. Dad watched Paddy's parachute open, and then it came twisted somehow and collapsed into itself.

My dad watched his best mate plummet to the ground. He said that Paddy must have had a premonition that his parachute wasn't going to open and, as far as he was concerned, he'd killed his best mate Paddy. I was born just after the Second World War, and my dad gave me my second Christian name of Paddy in his memory.

*

My dad had brought malaria back from the war so I don't know whether it was remorse for thinking he killed Paddy or the malaria mixed with booze that sent him off his head every Friday night. I was thirteen years old now and, for as long as I can remember, Friday nights were always the same. My dad would come home from work about six o'clock. He would have a wash, take his boots off and park himself in his chair next to the fire and eat the meal Mum put in front of him off his lap. After his meal, he would send me with two empty pop bottles to the 'Happy Wanderer' pub, about two hundred yards from our house. In the outdoor of the pub they would fill the pop bottles up with beer then put a sticky label over the cork. This was, I suppose, a deterrent to stop us kids from tasting the ale. This done, I would take the ale back to Dad, who would start drinking very early. Friday was payday for Dad and it was the only night he drank. We had a Rediffusion in our house; very few people had televisions in those days. The Rediffusion only had three channels, and my dad just put a channel on at random. He never really listened to it. I know Friday night was the night to listen to the demons in his head. God only knows what shit he saw in that terrible war. How many young men did he see getting slaughtered and maimed? How many young enemy soldiers did he kill? For the first hour or so of my dad drinking, he seemed quite amiable, and then after four or five more trips to the outdoor off licence, Mum took me to bed. She always gave me a cuddle and a kiss on my forehead telling me she loved me. I can remember the sadness that always seemed to be in her eyes these days.

'Thanks, Mum,' I said as she tucked me in bed. She just smiled, turned round and left my bedroom, closing the door behind her. I was just falling off to sleep when my dad kicked off. Bottles smashing against the wall, furniture (what bit we had) kicked all over the house and Mum crying. I had three older sisters and an older brother. I was the youngest, with five years between me and my younger sister. My three sisters, who had had enough of this shit, fucked off ages ago. My oldest brother I saw more than once battling with my dad on a Friday night, father and son. They hated each other and acted like sworn enemies. There were no holds barred. I saw my brother and dad butting and kicking the shit out of each other while my Mum looked on, crying. Blood all over the place. My brother was strong, but he wasn't a match for my dad. My brother would always be the one to leave the house until my dad fell asleep, then he would sneak back in, clean himself up and go to bed. My brother eventually had enough of this and, like my sisters, decided to leave home. He told Mum he was going to join the army. A few days later, bags packed, he gave Mum a big hug and then, turning to me, wrapped his arms round me and told me he loved me. Picking his bags up, he headed towards the door. He opened the door and stepped through it, then turning back round, he looked at Mum and said, 'Leave the bastard, you've had nothing but heartache and grief in your life, you deserve better.'

Then, turning, he closed the door behind him. Mum pulled me into her breast and cried uncontrollably. That would be the last time I would see my brother for a few years.

I could still hear furniture being kicked all over the place when Mum opened my bedroom door. She knew I was the only one who could calm him down when he was in this state. Grabbing my hand, she led me downstairs to Dad. As soon as he saw me he would calm down, pick me up and sit me on his knee on his chair next to the fire. He always called me his 'little mon'. He would hug me and after a little while we would fall asleep, Dad in a drunken stupor. Later, Mum would ease me from my father's arms and take me back to bed. This was the Friday night ritual until one day my mum, who had finally had enough told me she was going to divorce Dad and that she was going to move in with Alma, my big sister who lived in Leicestershire. I begged her not to divorce my dad, told her that I loved them both equally, but Mum was determined, asking me to go with her. I was now fourteen years of age and didn't want to leave my school mates, especially Fred. I told my mum tearfully that I was going to stay with Dad. Mum had already packed her bags while Dad was at work. She held me close to her and told me she loved me and that she would write to me often. Picking up her bags she left the house, and I cried like I'd never cried before. I'd never really had a family life and I had even less of one now. I had so much sadness and grief in my heart, it felt as though my whole world was falling apart around me. Just me and Dad now. I knew when he came home from work he would be devastated. It was quarter to six and I was looking out the window waiting to see Dad walking down the road from work. What was I going to tell him? I didn't have long to wait. In my grief, I forgot to make his dinner, but I knew that would be the last thing on his mind when I told him about Mum.

He came in the back door and on seeing me he said, 'Hello, my little mon, ew am yow?' Then he saw the tears in my eyes and asked, 'What's the matter'?

I could hardly speak. I was sobbing and my words wouldn't come out.

'Where is Mum'? he said.

I managed to blurt out, 'She's left you, Dad, and she's gone to live with Alma.'

He just looked at me, moved over to his chair, sat down and wept.

Dad still went to work, and every day after school I would come home and tidy the house and cook my dad's dinner. I could see the look of loss in my dad's eyes, and his drinking became more frequent, not just Friday nights anymore. I could see my dad's health start to deteriorate and it was breaking my heart. He really tried his best for me, but after enduring months of heartache and misery I told my dad that I, too, was leaving him. I was just a young kid and could not take any more. On turning fifteen years of age, I left school and I left Dad. In all his badness, he never raised a finger to me and I knew he loved me. He was going to die a lonely old man. I was so unhappy. What I wouldn't have given for a normal, happy family life.

I joined my mum at my big sister's house in Leicestershire. We wouldn't be there very long because my sister and George, her husband, had decided that they were going to emigrate to Australia. It was good to see my mum and sister again, and for the next twelve months or so I was quite happy, although I missed my dad and Fred.

I was just over sixteen years of age when I told my mum I wanted to join the army. She gave me her blessing and said she would sign my papers to join up. I passed my joining exams and medicals and on the 5th December 1962 I joined the Kings Shropshire Light Infantry in the junior soldiers regiment at Copthorn Barracks. The barracks were in the ancient market town of Shrewsbury in the heart of Shropshire. I didn't know it at the time, but for the next twenty-four years the army would be a big part of my family, and I would make friends that I would have for the rest of my life.

Army Days

I'd only been four months with the junior soldiers when I got my first taste of jankers. When the officers' or sergeants' mess cooks needed dogsbodies to scrub their pots and pans or spud bashing or any other menial job, they had a whole junior soldiers' wing to pick on. On going to meals, the provost staff would be at the entrance to the cook house checking for dirty hands or dirty *'hogging irons'. Just an excuse to get you in front of the old man who would dish out jankers. Then the cooks would have their dogsbodies.

Anyway, I was going for my dinner when this snotty lance corporal *RP done me for having a tiny crumb lodged between the tines of my fork.

'What's your name and number?' he barked.

I told him and he wrote my name and number down with a half-dozen other names of soldiers that he had nicked.

'Be outside the company office 0900 tomorrow,' he continued. 'You've lost your name.'

The following morning there were eight of us outside the company office, waiting to be marched in by the sergeant major. After about ten minutes the sergeant major turned up, saying, 'Right you lot, take your berets off.' We did as we were ordered and one by one got marched in to the old man, and everyone of us got seven days' jankers. Jankers, or restriction of privileges to give its right meaning, is when you finish your day's work at five. You go for your evening meal, then report to the guardroom by 1800 hours. Once there, you will be told by the provost staff where you will be 'slaving' for the next two hours, either the sergeants' or officers' mess. You finish this work at 2000 hours then report back to the guardroom. For the next hour and a half, we would be running backwards and forwards between our billets and the guardroom doing quick change parades. Each time we had to get into whatever dress they told us. Turn up in PT kit and, after inspection, twenty minutes to get changed into service dress or fatigues. It was just a way of fucking us about. At 2130 hours they would send us off to get into our best kit, full battle dress with our small packs on our backs, boots bulled, brasses shining. This was the last parade and we had to be spot on or we would get nicked again.

All of us outside the guardroom, 2200 hours, was the last parade, and it was always taken by the orderly officer and orderly sergeant, with a provost corporal on standby in case any of us got stuck in nick.

Standing to attention, getting inspected by the orderly *'Rupert' (orderly officer), when he looked at me and said, 'You've got Brasso on one of your buttons. Take his name, sergeant.'

'Yes, sir. Name, junior private?' said the sergeant.

'Junior Private H, sergeant,' I said. This would mean another seven days' jankers, another seven days without having a night off to go down town. I'd recently met a girl in town and had been going out with her for over a week before I got my first week's jankers. All the other lads finished off their week's jankers as I started my second week. I just couldn't get off these stinking jankers. It was my twenty-eighth day. It was the 2200 hours parade. If I got through this I would be able to get out with the lads and maybe see my girlfriend again, if she was still interested. I should get through this time. All the lads had helped me with my kit. One kid was brilliant at bulling boots and he got mine sparkling. No way the Rupert could get me for my boots. The lads had double-checked my kit, brasses, all shining, battle dress well ironed and small pack nice and tidy on my back.

Standing in line (there were only three of us tonight), when the Rupert got to me. He didn't even look at me and said, 'Take his name, sergeant.'

'Sir' I said, 'why are you taking my name?'

He looked aghast as though I'd got no right to question him. 'Because I'm taking it,' yelled the orderly officer.

'You can't take my name unless you tell me what for, sir.' I said.

'Sergeant, take his name for insubordination.'

'Yes sir.'

Right, I thought, here goes. I took my small pack off my back and threw it with all my might right through the large guardroom window. 'Now, sir,' I said, 'that's something to nick me for,' marching myself into jail before the provost corporal, jaw hanging open, lost for words, could do it.

I spent the rest of the night in the nick. At 0500 the next morning, the provost staff woke me up and doubled me to my room to get my washing and shaving kit, then doubled me back to the guardroom. I showered and shaved and got back into my best battle dress ready to see the old man. 0900, I got marched into the CO's office by the company sergeant major to find out my fate. Standing to attention in front of the old man's desk when the CO read my charge. 'You are charged with wilful damage in that you threw your small pack through the guardroom window, smashing it. How do you plead?'

'Guilty, sir,' I replied.

'Why did you do it?'

'Well, sir, it was my last day on jankers, my last parade after already doing twenty-eight days. I haven't left the camp for a month and I haven't seen my girlfriend all this time. All the lads had helped me with my kit and they all double-checked me to make sure I was okay. When the orderly officer took my name on the last parade, I asked him why was he taking my name and the twa— orderley officer couldn't tell me.' I saw the colonel bow his head to try and stop himself from smiling when I nearly called the orderly officer a twat. 'I thought I was going to get another seven days' jankers for nothing,' I continued. 'That's why I threw my small pack through the guardroom window. I thought I would give him something worthwhile to nick me for.'

The colonel looked up at me and said, 'The guardroom window is going to cost one pound, ten shillings and sixpence to repair. Your wage is ten shillings a week. You will pay half a crown a week until the window is paid for. Do you except my punishment?'

'Yes, sir,' I replied.

'March him out, sergeant major.'

'Yes, sir.'

I got marched out the old man's office and the sergeant major said, 'You were lucky there.'

'I know, sir,' I replied.

People seemed to leave me alone after that little episode. Everybody thought I was a nutter. I served just under eighteen months with the junior soldiers' regiment. It was like being back at school again. Twice a week we had to study English, Maths and General Studies. We all had to learn how to iron, because as the platoon sergeant said, our mothers weren't there to iron for us. We did lots of sport and weapon training. We all got taught how to strip, assemble and fire the *SMG (submachine gun), the *SLR (self-loading rifle) and also the Browning 9mm pistol. Also we learned how to map read and how to use a compass. All this learning would help me when I finally got to men's service. I knew I could take anything men's service threw at me when my time came. Junior soldiers was tough going, but we all got on with it. I made lots of friends in the juniors, some of which I still keep in touch with to this day.

On reaching 17½ years of age, I eventually joined the training company in the same barracks, but on the far side of the drill square, away from the junior soldiers' wing. As I expected, I flew through the training, learning more skills such as rock-climbing and abseiling. On completion of my training – 'passing out', as it was called – I got my first posting. I went to Plymouth, where I joined my new battalion in Seaton Barracks, Crownhill. I joined a company and was in 3 Platoon. I soon got to know all the lads. I was now an infantryman and quite proud of myself.

The RSM (regimental sergeant major) of our battalion had an RSM's drill parade every Saturday morning on the drill square, and if he was satisfied with our turnout he would stand the battalion down until first parade Tuesday morning. There would be a skeleton party to look after the barracks while we were all on a long weekend.

At 0800 the whole battalion lined up in three ranks on

the drill square. Everyone dressed in best kit – 'No 2s' was our best uniform. Bulled boots and brasses on our belts gleaming. We were all standing to attention as the RSM and the provost staff walked among the ranks. After about ten minutes, the RSM marched to the front of the battalion. 'Stand at Ease!' he yelled. The whole battalion as one stood at ease. The RSM continued, 'Company commanders and company sergeant majors fall out.' The company commanders and sergeant majors came to attention, turned to their right and marched off the square. The RSM yelled, 'Front rank, take your hats off. Middle rank, take your left boot off. Rear rank, remove your belts.'

'Fuck me,' my mate next to me whispered as we stooped to take off our left boots.

'What's up, Ken?' I said.

'I'm fucked,' he whispered. 'Bang goes my long weekend.' He took his boot off, looking over at me and shaking his head from side to side. I couldn't help a stifled laugh. Ken was a teddy boy when he wasn't in uniform, and he was wearing his teddy boy socks: bright pink socks, which the razz man spotted as soon as Ken's boot came off. The razz man yelled at two of his provost staff, 'Put that Moron in nick. Get twinkle toes off my parade square.' The provost staff ran over and, one each side of Ken, took him hobbling to nick. About ten squaddies got done for one thing or another. This wasn't bad compared to some RSM's parades of the past.

Long weekend over, we were all back in camp. I bumped into me mate Ken and said, 'What happened in nick?' He said he'd been in the sergeants' and officers' mess all weekend, spud-bashing and cleaning pots and pans. 'Tough luck, mate,' I said. 'We're all going out Thursday for a couple of beers, you can drown your sorrows then, mate.'

Thursday night came round fast. Ken and I and a half-dozen mates went for a drink down the local pub. We were all sitting around telling jokes and generally getting pissed when another of our mates, who was the company clerk, came over to join us. Sitting down, he said, 'Hey lads, have you heard the rumours?'

'What rumours?' piped up Ken.

'The battalion is going to Singapore for three years,' said Tom, the company clerk.

'Bloody hell, that's great news,' said Ken, 'if it's true.'

'Where the fuck is Singapore?' asked Joe.

'Fucked if I know,' said Tom.

All the lads seemed to be pleased at this news and the beer started to flow more freely.

Closing up time, we all finished our beers and headed for the chippy across the road from the pub. One of the lads was so pissed he had to be propped up by a couple of the other lads. After we all got our meals we were all walking down the road towards our barracks, feeding our faces, when all of a sudden, this geezer came racing around a corner. He was carrying a bag under his arm, he had training shoes on and he was wearing a balaclava over his head. Apart from that, he was stark bollock naked. All of a sudden, two coppers came running around the same corner, chasing the streaker. We all burst out laughing. I didn't think the cops would catch that streaker, he was so fucking fast.

Arriving back at barracks, we all went to our rooms, stripped off and got into our beds. Getting into my bed I said, 'Fuck me whose shite? It stinks in here.' There was a couple of titters and the room fell silent apart from the farting and snoring.

0600. The sound of the bugler blowing reveille started, waking us all up. I sat up in bed, rubbing my eyes. I had a mouth like a whore's handbag and a tongue like my grannie's fur coat. I smelt shit.

There was a strong smell of shit. 'Where is it coming from?' I wondered. I looked over to Jack's bed, the guy who was pissed out of his head last night. He got out of bed and he was covered in crap. He had it all over himself. One of the other lads who had been watching Jack shouted, 'You dirty bastard, you've shit your bed!' Jack, standing there in his skiddies, looked aghast. He grabbed a towel and soap and ran towards the showers. All the lads were awake now and complaining about the stench.

We all started making our beds and sorting ourselves out ready for breakfast. After breakfast we would all be going for a five-mile tab (fast march carrying packs). We were all young men and after a good night out we could still do a five-miler, albeit with a hangover. Jack had only been to the showers for ten minutes when he came back into the room saying, 'I never shit myself.' He had a towel round his waist and he was holding his skiddies in front of him with his outstretched arm. He said, 'I had no shit round my arse when I took my skiddies off, and the inside of my skiddies were clean. One of you dirty bastards shit in my bed, and when I find the twat I'm going to kill him.'

'No one in this platoon would do a shit trick – shit trick, haha, get it? – like that,' said Joe, another lad in the platoon.

'The phantom shitter must be back,' said Curly, as Jack

was rolling up his bed sheets to throw in the bin. A couple of years ago, the phantom shitter was shitting all over the place, and he never got caught. It just stopped happening and everyone thought the shitter must have been de-mobbed or something.

'Fuck, what a load of bollocks,' said Ken.

We all made our beds, shaved, showered and just got on with our morning ritual.

0700 hours. The bugler sounded 'cookhouse' on his bugle. That's another thing all infantryman had to learn, all the bugle calls. You had reveille to wake you up, cookhouse to tell you it's meal time, call for sick parade, jankers, first post, last post. All kinds of calls had to be learnt.

The barracks were in sight. We were all only firing on one lung, running, coughing, snot running down our noses. The corporal in charge of the five-miler was taking the piss. He was trying to teach us a lesson for being on the ale last night. He was really beasting us. Entering the barracks, we all had to do one lap of the sports field; this made the run exactly five miles measured out by the battalion's physical training instructor (PTI). There's also a ten-mile run-and-walk and a twenty-five-miler. One by one we finished the run, a couple of the lads having a *'kit check' (puke) at the finish. When we were all over the line, the corporal marched us back to our billets for a shower. Finishing my shower, I went back to the billet and saw Johnny, another one of the lads, sitting on his bed! 'Hi Johnny, where have you been? I never saw you on the five-miler.'

'Yeh, I missed it, I had to go sick.'

'What for?' I asked.

'I've got a sore arse, grapes hanging out my ring, and they are killing me.'

I started laughing.

'It's no joke, H. The MO asked me what was wrong with me and I told him I think I've got haemorrhoids. The MO bent me over, checked my ring and after his examination, do you know what the cheeky bastard said, H?'

'I'm sure you are going to tell me, John.'

Johnny said, 'The doctor told me I didn't have haemorrhoids. He said officers get haemorrhoids, senior ranks get piles and junior ranks get sore arses, and I've got the latter, the cheeky twat.'

The months were flying by now, and Curly was right about the phantom shitter showing up again, or else someone was copying him. One guy got up one morning, put his foot into his boot only to find someone had shit in it. Over the months, the shitter was becoming famous throughout the battalion.

He even got put on 'Part 1 Orders' telling everyone in the battalion where the shitter had struck. On the loo chain, some squaddie got a hand full of shite when he pulled it. Under someone's pillow, inside a squaddie's locker, in some poor bastard's coat pocket, just to name a few.

Thursday night, me and half a dozen lads down the local getting sloshed. The main topics of conversation being the phantom shitter, the forthcoming tour of Singapore and such. Kenny said, 'Do you remember that streaker we saw a couple of months ago, H?'

'Yeh,' I said, 'what of it?'

'Well, he's as famous as the phantom shitter. He's even been in the local rag. For the last couple of months on a Thursday night, he's never failed to do a streak through the village. Always getting chased by cops and according to the local paper no one's got any idea who he is.'

'Hey, its Thursday' said Tom. 'Wonder if he'll streak tonight.'

A few laughs and the conversation, jokes and general banter resumed.

I liked these lads. I liked my army life and I knew I would stay in for as long as I could. I signed on for twenty-two years, so it's a good job. I liked it. It had become my family.

Finishing our beers, we headed for the chippy, about fifteen squaddies packing the chippy out when someone shouted, 'The show's on, lads!' We all looked out the chippy window and there was the streaker running faster than I last remembered. He had four coppers chasing him, and it looked like one of the coppers was as fast as the streaker – the copper was almost on him. We all clapped and cheered as the streaker ran past. 'Go for it, lad!' someone yelled. 'Nice arse!' someone else piped up.

We all had a bloody good laugh. There's never a dull moment in the army, I thought to myself.

The battalion had been informed that we would be going to Singapore and that the advance party would be leaving Plymouth on the 8th September 1966, followed by the bulk of the battalion on the 1st Oct 1966. So there it is, in a couple of months' time I would be doing my first tour abroad, and I was really looking forward to it.

Rsm's Drill Parade

0800 Saturday morning, the battalion all lined up on the square. This was the last RSM's parade for a while because the battalion would be so busy preparing for Singapore. Everyone standing to attention, the company commanders and company sergeant majors were excused this parade. Just the platoon Ruperts and sergeants in charge of each company. The razz man and his half-dozen provost staff started walking up and down the files of soldiers, glaring into their eyes, not saying a word. The whole battalion was silent. One of the provost staff got to me and gave me an intimidating look. 'What the fuck's this about?' I wondered. He then moved on, glaring at one squaddie after another. I'm sure the RSM and his staff must have given everyone on parade the eyeball treatment.

After about thirty minutes the RSM and his staff marched out to the front of the battalion, still glaring. He had not said a word while this was going on. His head moved from side to side as he scanned all the troops in front of him. 'Right,' yelled the RSM (silence broken), 'there's one vile, horrible, low life scumbag amongst you.' The RSM waited for this to sink in before continuing. 'The phantom shitter has struck again!' screamed the RSM, veins sticking out of his neck, eyes bulging. A ripple of laughter ran through the ranks. 'Shut the fuck up!' yelled the razz man.

Ken, standing next to me, whispered, 'I don't know how I'm going to stop myself from laughing, H.'

'Shut the fuck up, Ken,' I said, trying to suppress my laughter, 'or we'll both end up in nick.'

'The phantom shitter,' continued the razz man, 'has shit in A Company Commanders in tray.'

'Fuck me,' said Ken, putting his hand over his mouth. I was in the middle file of our company and I was watching the squaddie's shoulders in front of me shaking.

It wouldn't take much, I thought, to get the whole battalion breaking out in fits of laughter. Eyes still bulging, veins in his neck still sticking out, the RSM raged, 'And the cheeky bastard had the gall to mark it URGENT.' Ruperts, sergeants, corporals, the whole battalion broke down in fits of laughter.

'Get the fuck off my square,' yelled the razz man, throwing a fit. 'Go on, the lot of you, fuck off.' The razz man was still throwing a fit as the whole battalion ran off the square, squealing with laughter.

Singapore was getting closer now, and the whole battalion, less the rear party, had been given two weeks' leave to see family and friends and say their goodbyes. When leave was over, there was only a fortnight to go, and all the married personnel were busy cleaning out their married quarters ready for 'march out'. The whole camp was a hive of activity. Getting ready for the move.

All the guys in the local. This would be our last Thursday night before deployment. Some of the *'pads' (married personnel) had their wives with them and some of the lads' girlfriends had turned up. It would be a mixture of feelings at the end of this night, what with the lads saying goodbye to their girlfriends and such.

Anyway, at the moment everyone seemed to be having a good time. Ron, one of my married mates, and his wife Suzy had popped round for a few drinks and came over and sat next to me.

'What do you think of the posting?' I asked Suzy.

'Three years in Singapore, a holiday paid for by the tax man!' she said, laughing. 'What do you think, H?'

'Yeh,' I said, 'I'm looking forward to it myself.' I'd known Ron and Suzy from when I first joined the battalion, and we had become good friends. The night was coming to an end and everyone started to drink up. Some of the lads had already gone to the chippy to beat the queue.

'Come on, Ron, Suzy, I'll treat you to a fish supper.'

'Not a bad idea,' Suzy said. 'I'm starving now.'

We finished our ale, got our jackets and headed for the chippy. We were all queueing up in the chippy – it was packed out, you could hardly move – when, all of a sudden, the chippy door got shoved open and the streaker barged through the crowd, screaming, 'Block the door, lads, don't let the fuzz in!' He whipped his hood and shoes off and started pulling clothes out of the bag he was carrying. We were all in shock, for when he whisked his balaclava off, we all recognised him as Dennis, the battalion's cross country champion. Everyone was laughing as half a dozen lads casually leant against the chippy door as the fuzz were trying to get in. Dennis, in the meantime, was trying to get dressed, hidden by the crowd of squaddies, wives and girlfriends. I noticed a couple of the girls trying to get a good look at Dennis's tackle. He was a big lad. The fuzz finally got in the chippy.

Dennis nearly made it. He threw his hood and bag over

the chippy counter and was just about to put his trainers on when the fuzz got him. Two of the coppers grabbed Dennis by the scruff of the neck and dragged him out to a waiting police car. The whole chippy broke out in peals of laughter. The cops were out in force tonight, they must have blocked all his escape routes, that's why, I assume, he tried to escape in the chippy. Fuck me, I really enjoyed this army life, it was a laugh a minute. When the cops found out Dennis was a soldier and due to go out to Singapore in a week's time, they let him off.

When Dennis got marched in front of the old man, he got a hefty fine. He also got the piss taken out of him for months to come.

A few days before we were due to fly out to Singapore, the platoon sergeant got us all together in one of our rooms. The sergeant told us a medic would be coming shortly to give us all a little chat. 'He's due at 1400' he said. I looked at my watch: ten minutes to wait.

At exactly 1400 hours, the medic arrived, carrying a small rucksack. 'Hello lads' he greeted us. 'This talk will only take a few minutes, it's just to give you a little insight into Singapore.' He sat down on one of the beds facing us. 'I'm here to give you a couple of warnings just to make you aware of some of the dangers of the Far East. When you get to Singapore, every one of you will spend two weeks at the jungle warfare school (JWS), which is across the causeway, just inside Malaya, in a place call Johor Bahru. You will be taught jungle warfare and how to survive in the jungle. I'm here to warn you how to survive the sun and malaria. The sun will burn you to a crisp. It's hot, damn hot, so you will treat it with respect. It's recommended that you don't stay out in the sun more than thirty minutes before finding shade. All of us here in England are lucky to get two weeks of sun a year. Out there, it's almost every day, apart from the monsoons. Right lads,' the medic said, opening his rucksack, 'I'm going to issue you all with a week's worth of Paludrine. These Paludrine tablets are to protect you from malaria. You will all start taking these pills from today.'

One pill to be taken once a day. It's your duty to make sure you do this. Out in Singapore, you might be away from the battalion or on leave, so you make sure you have enough Paludrine to take with you. It's impossible to get malaria if you take your tablet every day.'

The medic stood up and went round each soldier giving them exactly seven tablets, saying, 'Remember, lads, if you end up with malaria, it's because you have missed taking your Paludrine.' After each soldier got his tablets, the medic stood in front of us saying, 'When you get to Singapore you will get a week to acclimatise, to get used to the heat and sun. Any questions, lads?'

'What about Paludrine for our families?' one of the pads asked.

'The families officer and his staff will today be visiting all married quarters with an envelope for each quarter with instructions, information and warnings about the sun and malaria. It's each individual family's responsibility to ensure all their family take Paludrine and to protect themselves from the sun.'

'Thanks, Doc,' said the pad (all medics are called Doc).

'Any more questions? No? Okay, lads, have a good tour in the Far East.'

On the 8th October 1966, our company was driven to Brize Norton in coaches. We would fly from Brize Norton to Singapore in a TriStar Airliner.

Singapore

The Lockheed TriStar touched down at Changi airport. It had been a long old haul, but we were finally in Singapore. The aircraft slowly taxied over to the disembarkment area and came to a halt. Looking out the aircraft window, I could see it was a glorious day. This was my first time ever in a foreign country. It was really an exciting time for me. After about twenty minutes, we all started to disembark. As I got to the aircraft's exit the heat from outside washed over me. It was a lovely feeling, like walking into a sauna. At the bottom of the aircraft's steps was a couple of our advance party members there to escort us. They led us into the terminal where we would eventually pick up our luggage from the carousel. After collecting our luggage we went through customs and then to our awaiting coaches.

The coach trip to Changi Barracks took just over thirty minutes due to the amount of traffic on the roads. The coaches filed past the guardroom and turned onto a massive drill square. Kenny, sitting next to me, said, 'Changi Barracks was a big prisoner-of-war camp during World War Two, when the Japanese invaded Malaya and Singapore. This is where they kept all the prisoners of war.'

'I bet a lot of shit happened here, Ken,' I said.

'Lots of atrocities, mate,' he said. 'I've read books about this place. You wouldn't believe the shit the POWs went through.'

After debussing and collecting our luggage we were shown the way to our billets. The lads doing all the organising were two full corporals and a lance corporal from the quartermaster's (QM's) staff. After about an hour we were all settled down in our bunks and billets. All the pads were taken in separate coaches to their married quarters. For the next week we would be acclimatising and we would be getting issued with our Far East uniforms and equipment. I couldn't believe this heat. The platoon was lined up outside the colour sergeant's stores, marching up one at a time and signing for our kit the colour sergeant issued us. Almost everything came in threes – three shirts, three pairs of shorts, three pairs of trousers, all lightweight kit (LWK). We got issued with a set of Australian lightweight kit, we got told it was good gear and we would get taught how to use it at the Jungle Warefare School at Johor Bahru. I stuffed all my kit into my kitbag and took it back to my room where I unpacked it and put it in my locker.

We were also issued with a large knife. We called it a 'Panga'. It came in a sheath that also housed a sharpening stone. It could be worn on your belt and was used for cutting through the thick Malay jungle. Each soldier had a toddle rope. It had a piece of hard wood at one end and a loop at the other. Each soldier's toddle rope could be joined together by slipping the wood through the loop of each rope. This would help should we need a length of rope to get up or down steep jungle hills or crossing small rivers.

It was Friday afternoon and our platoon sergeant told us we could have the weekend off to explore Singapore. Beaver, one of our mates from the advance party who had already been to Singapore half a dozen times, arranged to take Ken and I down town to show us the ropes and dens of iniquity.

1000 hours Saturday morning, Beaver met Ken and I in the NAAFI. 'Hi, lads,' he greeted us. 'Come on, let's get a taxi.' We left the camp gates and got into one of the many taxis that was always parked outside the camp. It was only 1000 hours, but the sun was already scorching. Beaver told the taxi driver to take us to the Tiger Balm Gardens.

'Fuck me,' I said to Beaver, 'I know it's too early to drink, but who wants to walk round friggin' flower gardens?'

'Wait till you see these, mate, they are not flower gardens, you've seen nothing like it,' he said.

The taxi pulled up outside the gardens and we paid our fare and got out the taxi, Beaver leading the way. The gardens were a maze of footpaths. There were thick shrubbery and trees either side of the paths and there were statues everywhere, some out in the open, some hidden in the bushes – you had to look hard to see some of them. 'Fuck me,' Ken said, 'look at that one!' A guy with a terrified look on his face was tied and stretched between two trees; sat on his haunches, with a manic grin on his face, was a devil pulling the guy's intestines out. Next to the devil were two men in fits of laughter.

'Bloody hell, Beaver, what's all this about?' I said.

'I've seen almost every statue in this garden,' he replied, 'and just when you think you can't see anything worse, something more evil pops up. Come on, I'll show you a few more.' All the statues were nude or semi-nude, and those that did have clothes on were dressed in oriental clothing. The blood and the gore was unbelievable. There was a group of statues squatting around a corpse; one female had a spoon with an eyeball in it, about to put it into a baby's mouth. One guy had an intestine in his mouth, sucking it up like spaghetti, while another had his hand inside the corpse's stomach, foraging around for who-knows-what. It was an unbelievable place, and the farther you walked into the gardens the worse the atrocities seemed to get. It was a place of torture, pain and devils, but I'm glad Beaver brought us to see it. I was twenty years old now and I never knew anything like this existed, and I knew Singapore and Malaya would have a lot more surprises and experiences for me.

The next place Beaver took us to was Bugis Street. He said, 'You have never been to Singapore till you've been here. All the squaddies call it Boogie Street.' We were walking among the many stalls, watching all the hustle and bustle.

'Bloody hell,' said Ken. 'I've never seen so many beautiful girls in one place, there's loads of them.'

Beaver said, 'you want to be careful if you fancy chatting one up. Most of them girls are boys. They are called kaitais or something like that, or ladyboys.'

Boogie Street was a mass of sprawling shacks and brick-built buildings. The smell of the many spices filled the air, curry being the stronger of the smells. There were many tables and hundreds of chairs strung out each side of the road. There wasn't room for traffic down there, apart from the many rickshaws. Pretty much every other building was a restaurant of sorts. I wouldn't even hazard a guess at some of the stuff that they were cooking and selling. There were literally hundreds of people sitting around the tables eating their food and looking like they were enjoying it. There were hundreds more people walking around in all directions. I'd never seen so many people in one place like this before. This must have been the main meeting place of Singapore.

The ladyboys, or 'kaitais', were everywhere; they seemed to hang round in small groups dressed up in their finery, overacting their alter egos. I just could not believe they were boys; some of them could, I'm sure, pass themselves off as women, enter a beauty contest and end up winning it. After about an hour of taking in the sights, Beaver said, 'Come on, lads, I'll bring you back here later for some food. The curry here is second to none. It's time for a few beers now.' There were hundreds of bars all over the place, but Beaver told us the one he was taking us to was a bit special. Entering the bar was like walking out of a fire into a fridge, the large fans spinning on the ceiling bringing welcome respite from the heat. It took a few moments for our eyes to adjust to the darkness of the bar after the bright sunlight outside. A minute or so after entering the bar, several girls came over to us. A couple of them speaking in pidgin English, saying, 'Hello, Johnny, you buy me a beer?' They took us by the arms and led us to a large table where we all sat down.

It was quite dark in the bar – you could just about see the tables next to us – and I noticed there were very few other customers in the bar. Ken sat opposite me with a girl sitting either side of him with their arms draped over his shoulders, then sat Beaver with a girl putting her arms around his neck and kissing him on his cheek.

'I can see you've been here before, Beaver,' I said.

'You've got that right, H,' he said.

I was sitting at the now crowded table, and I also had girls sitting next to me.

'Are these girls ... girls?' asked Kenny.

'Yes, mate. There are no ladyboys here.'

A couple more girls came over to our table carrying a tray each with bottles of tiger beer on them. The girls handed us each a beer and helped themselves to one each.

'Nine dollars, Johnny,' one girl said.

Beaver gave her ten, saying, 'Keep the change.'

We all settled down, drinking our beers and chatting away to the girls when I looked across the table at Kenny. He had the most stupid grin on his face. I looked at the two girls either side of him, both had their arms round his neck and their other arms under the table. All of a sudden, the girl next to me put her hand between my legs under the table and started to fondle me. I hadn't been with a girl for ages and got an instant hard-on. The girl unbuttoned my fly, took my cock out and started to masturbate me. I then must have had the same stupid grin on my face as Kenny sitting opposite me. After a few seconds of the girl wanking me, I let out a suppressed groan and came. It must have taken all of thirty seconds for me to come. Beaver and Kenny soon followed suit, almost coming at the same time.

'Bloody hell, lads, I've never experienced anything like that in my life,' I said.

Beaver stood up closing his fly and said, 'Excuse us, ladies. Come on, boys, let's go to the bogs to clean ourselves off.'

In the bogs, scrubbing our cocks and cleaning the sperm off our keks, I said to Beaver, 'I wouldn't shag any of them even with yours, or if I had a johnny as thick as a Dunlop tyre. You would end up with the screaming abdabs.'

'That's why I come here,' said Beaver. 'A little wank never hurt anybody. Welcome to one of the many "winky wanky bars".' We all burst out laughing.

After we finished our ablutions, we rejoined the girls at the table. I ordered another round of beers and we chatted to the girls. The girl next to me was after seconds – it didn't take long for her to get my cock out again. I think I lasted about a minute this time. When she'd finished wanking me, I went back to the bogs to clean myself up. Returning to the table I lifted my Tiger to my lips and emptied the bottle. 'Come on, lads, I'm, drained dry, my sack's empty and it needs a rest.' Beaver and Kenny stood up, finished off their beers and gave their girls a little cuddle.

'Right H, say bye to your bird, let's go.'

God, I thought to myself, I'm so naïve.

As we left the bar a blast of warm air hit us. We visited a few more bars and soaked up the sun's rays in a couple of outside bars. I loved it out here.

'Right, lads,' said Beaver, 'let's go a bit more upmarket. We'll have to jump a taxi, I don't fancy a three-mile walk in this heat.'

'Where're we going?' said Ken.

'Raffles,' said Beaver.

'That name rings a bell with me,' said Ken.

'What is it?' I asked.

'It's a big, posh hotel that used to be frequented by the rich and famous. Twenty or thirty years ago, the likes of us wouldn't have got through the front door.'

The taxi pulled up outside Raffles and we all got out. I looked at the hotel; it was certainly an impressive looking building. We entered the hotel to the welcome blast of cool air coming from the many fans I could see all round the large room we were in. Beaver said, 'I'll go and get the beers, you two have a look round.' I noticed a plaque hanging on a wall giving information about the hotel. It was a colonial style building, built in 1887. It had a fourteen-foot ceiling, one hundred and three rooms over three floors, all the many carpets were handmade, covering the teak wood floors. Its address was 1 Beach Road, Singapore. Everywhere you looked was sheer opulence; I had never been in a building like this. Kenny and I joined Beaver at the bar. Beaver pointed out old photographs on the wall behind the bar saying, 'That's just some of the VIPs that have stayed in the hotel over the years.' There were pictures of film stars, rock stars, prime ministers and royalty. The hotel must have been even more impressive twenty years ago.

After Raffles we got a taxi back to Boogie Street to get something to eat. Beaver said he knew a good restaurant that sold a good curry. The restaurant was called Zam Zam's, and it was very popular. Beaver continued saying as far as he knew no one had ever got Singapore Singe or Delhi Belly after eating there. Arriving at Zam Zam's, the three of us got a small table where we could eat our food and watch the hustle and bustle of Boogie Street. Zam Zam's was more like a large shack than a restaurant, but it was packed with people enjoying their food. A waiter came over to our table and took our order. We all decided on chicken curry along with three more Tigers. The beer and curry didn't take long in coming, and when I tasted the curry I said, 'Fuck me, this is bloody hot, but good.'

'Yeh,' agreed Kenny as we all tucked in.

Finishing my curry, I said to Beaver, 'You were right there, mate, that was bloody good shite, I just hope I don't wake up tomorrow with Rangoon Ring.'

'Naa, you will be okay, it's good stuff here.'

After a couple more beers, we jumped a taxi and headed back to our barracks. My first memorable outing in Singapore over.

Our platoon was all acclimatised now and we were all preparing for ten days' jungle training at Johor Bahru. It's the jungle warfare school and is situated in Malaya, just across the causeway that separated Singapore from Malaya.

*

Monday morning, the start of our ten-day exercise, there was two three-ton wagons on the square ready to take us to the JWS. Sergeant Jools gave the order to embus. We all clambered aboard the trucks; we were all dressed in full jungle greens, carrying our full jungle kit and carrying our rifles and guns. The drivers of the wagons, two Royal Core of Transport (RCT) lads, put the tail boards of the wagons up, making sure they were secured. Sergeant Jools got in the front of one cab, and Second Lieutenant Garry, the platoon Rupert, got into the other. The RCT lads started their trucks and made their way out of camp. The two trucks were rolling along the causeway; it wouldn't be long now till we got to the JWS. After about forty minutes, we reached our destination. We debussed next to a large sports field, which ran along the edge of the jungle. The heat was already making us all sweat and the noises coming out the jungle were unbelievable. Waiting for us was a Gurkha full corporal, one of the permanent staff at the JWS. He saluted our Rupert, saying 'Good morning, sir. I will escort your platoon to your accommodation, if you will follow me.'

'Thank you, corporal.'

The Rupert and platoon sergeant had their own bunks. The rabble (us) had two large huts. There were three bunks at the end of the accommodation huts; these were for the corporals. There was an ablution block in between our huts. The huts had solid walls about three feet high and then it was steel mesh to the roof. This was to keep the huts ventilated so we wouldn't fry in the heat. The huts had rows of steel-framed beds on either side of the room, and each bed had a mattress on them; we had brought our own mosquito nets. There were also three large fans, which were blowing welcome cold air around the room. Each bed had a large locker next to it, also a small bedside cabinet. We all started to unpack when Sergeant Jools came into the room saying, 'Leave what you are doing, grab your rifles and get fell in outside the block.' We all got fell in, in three ranks, and the sergeant said that we wouldn't be needing rifles for the first five days, so we were going to put them in the armoury. 'Stand ready,' he barked. 'To your left, quick march.' It was only a five-minute march to the armoury. After all our weapons were secured in the armoury, Sergeant Jools said, 'Right, lads, go back to your rooms and you can use the rest of today to get your kit sorted out. Breakfast tomorrow is 0700, I want you all in full jungle kit at 0800 ready for our first lesson, so don't be getting pissed tonight in the—'

BOOM

'What the fuck was that?' said the sergeant. We all looked in the direction of the loud bang. A small cloud of smoke could be seen rising out of some shrub at the edge of the jungle. 'It must be someone training,' said the sergeant. 'It sounded like a thunderflash to me. Anyway, before I was rudely interrupted, I was going to say don't get pissed in the NAAFI tonight, and be on your best behaviour. We aren't the only ones here – there are some Engineers, RCT, medics and I've seen lots of Gurkhas knocking around. So if you don't want your balls cut off with a kukri, behave yourselves.'

All the barracks and camps in the Far East had wallahs. They were all local people. The char wallah sold tea, coffee, sandwiches and such. The doby wallah did the laundry, the money wallah lent you a few bob when you were skint – if you borrowed ten dollars, you would have to pay eleven dollars back, not too bad. The char wallah was handy: you could always get something to eat up till 2300 hours when he closed. If you were skint, you could also run a tab up with him.

It was 2000 hours and we were all sitting around in our huts, the fans doing their jobs, blowing welcome cool air through the room. We had all got our kit sorted out. A few of us who didn't go to dinner had paid a visit to the char wallah and were busy eating sandwiches and drinking tea. We had already arranged with each other to go to the NAAFI at 2100 hours for a pint. By going as late as this, we thought we wouldn't have the time to get pissed because the NAAFI closed at 2230 hours. Corporal Tenwell entered our room and made his way over to where we were all sitting. Corporal Tenwell was our platoon full corporal and he was a stickler for discipline, in other words a right twat; he wasn't very popular at all. Just as he was about to sit down, he slipped on a slice of cheese someone had dropped on the floor. It was like slow motion: his feet went shooting up in the air until his body was almost horizontal. Then he came crashing down on one of the beds, his spine, from top to bottom, scraping against the steel edge of the bed. We all burst out laughing. He was sat down with both arms behind him, hands on the side of the bed trying to lift himself up. The lot of us were howling with laughter.

'Hellllp meeee!' cried the corporal.

None of us could move to help him, we were pissing ourselves.

'Pleeease helllp meee,' the corporal pleaded again.

A couple of the lads, still laughing, went over to him and lifted him to his feet. One of the lads lifted the corporal's shirt to look at his back. He had a nasty-looking scrape right down his spine, which caused more laughter when we saw it.

'Can you walk, corporal'? Joe asked, taking his arm and walking him down the length of our hut. He started off hobbling, painful sounds coming out his gob, almost wailing. After Joe walked him up and down the hut a couple of times he was alright.

'Fuck me, that hurt,' whinged the corporal, 'and thanks for the sympathy, you bunch of morons.' Having said that, he turned round and gingerly made his way out of the room.

'What the fuck did he come in here for in the first place?' laughed Kenny.

It was almost 2100 hours. 'Let's go to the NAAFI,' said Ken.

'Good idea, mate,' said Joe.

We all got up off our pits and made our way to the NAAFI. Walking up the road, running next to the open monsoon drains, I thought to myself, 'I wouldn't like to fall in that during the monsoons. You would get swept away to the swamps and end up on the menu for all kinds of creatures.' It was a lovely warm evening filled with the noises of the jungle. It's as though every creature comes out at night to hunt.

As we walked into the NAAFI we saw two of our lads, Curly and Johnny, already there with a couple of almost-empty beers in front of them. They were pissing themselves with laughter. We all got a Tiger each and joined them at their table.

'What the fuck you two laughing at?' I said.

Curly, slapping the table, could hardly talk through bouts of laughter and blurted out, 'Do you remember that "Boom" we heard earlier?' He was still tittering away.

'Yea, what about it?' said Joe.

'You know them thunder boxes?'

'What the fuck's a thunder box?' interrupted Kid.

'It's a makeshift shithouse,' continued Curly. 'Imagine a big oblong box with four or five holes in it, big enough to plonk your arse on.' More laughter. 'Well, it's like that with normally a corrugated tin roof on it and hessian cloth draped between each hole to give you a bit of privacy. All this is over a pit where your shit goes. Well, haa haa...' Another fit of laughter. 'Fuck me, this fuckin med, ha ha, med, hee heee, fuckin' medic was sitting on the ha haa, I can't help it ...' We were all laughing now. '... shithouse, minding his own business, he hee, when some twat threw a thunder flash down one of the bog holes ... me guts are killing me!'

'Carry on, for fuck's sake, Curly,' said Kid, laughing.

'The explosion caused the shit to fly up through the bog holes. It flew up, ha haa, it flew up through the hole where the medic was sitting. The shit flew up the medic's arse and bollox. It went right up his chest, hitting him under his chin and going up his nostrils.' The whole place erupted in laughter. 'The medic came staggering out of the thunder box covered in shite.'

Laughter subsiding, Curly continued, 'The prat who threw the thunderflash down the bog could have blown the medic's balls off, but the only thing that was hurt was his pride.' More laughter. 'He had to go to the MT yard's wash-down point to get hosed down then back to his own medical centre to get disinfected.'

'Who threw the fuckin thunderflash?' said Tom, the company clerk.

'No one knows.'

'Perhaps it was the phantom shitter looking for a new way to play with shite,' someone piped up.

'It's a good job it wasn't you sitting on the shitter, Johnny, it would have blown your piles off,' said Kenny. More laughter, this time at Johnny's expense.

'There's some nutters around here besides us,' I said.

*

Twenty minutes before parade the following morning, the platoon sergeant came into our room saying, 'Dress for this morning is jungle greens, belt, hats and water bottles. We won't be needing any of our other kit until after lunch. The lesson won't be in the classroom but on the far side of the sports field, next to the edge of the jungle.'

We all got ready and fell in on the road outside our blocks. Corporal Tenwell marched us all over to where we were to have our lesson, the platoon sergeant and Rupert following on behind us. Waiting for us in front of a trestle table was a Gurkha full corporal. Corporal Tenwell halted us just in front of the Gurkha and kept us standing to attention. The, Gurkha saluted our Rupert, who returned the compliment, saying, 'Thank you, corporal.'

The Gurkha, who spoke perfect English, said, 'Could you all sit in a semi-circle under the shade of those trees facing me.'

We all complied.

The corporal introduced himself, saying, 'I'm Corporal Shirisha, and I will be taking today's lessons. OK, lads, this lesson is about some of the things you can eat in the jungle and how to treat water to make it safe to drink. We teach this on the off chance you get lost in the jungle. You will then have knowledge of how to survive.' The Gurkha looked at us. He then bent down and scooped some twigs and dead leaves up in his hand. Straightening back up again, he said, 'You can eat anything in the jungle ...' He then put the dead leaves and twigs in his mouth and started to chew them. We all looked at him, shocked. After a couple of seconds' chewing, he spat the twigs and leaves out of his mouth saying, '... if you want to die.' He then opened his water bottle, took a swig of water, rinsed his mouth and spat out the water. Bloody hell, he's sure got our attention, I thought. 'Right, about the water you can drink in the "hulu". Before you go into the hulu you will all be issued with water purifying tablets and a Millbank bag. You will need one tablet for one full water bottle. It's best if you purify your water overnight – this gives time for the tablet to take effect. The time for purification is six hours. There's all kinds of shit that lives in the streams and mangrove, but if you use your tablets you will be okay. Never, ever drink straight from the streams. In some parts of the hulu, the only water you will find will be murky or muddy, which is not fit to drink unless treated.'

The Gurkha then lifted up a fire bucket from behind

the trestle table. He handed it to Jack, who was sat on the end of the semi- circle, saying, 'Show the contents of the bucket to the platoon.' Jack stood up and walked around the lads, showing them the muddy, murky water in the bucket. Jack then returned the bucket to the Gurkha. 'Right, lads, if this is the only water you can find, you have to clean it up before it's drinkable. This is where you use this.' He lifted up a bag about a foot long and eight inches wide off the table behind him. Holding the bag out in front of him, he said, 'This is a "Millbank bag". It's made of a porous canvas, and as you can see it's sealed to a slanted point at the bottom and it's got a loop at the top. This is a slow process, to get the shit out of the water, but it works.'

He walked over to a tree a few feet away, carrying the fire bucket and Millbank bag. He hung the bag on a branch and filled it with the murky water out of the bucket; he then put his water bottle mug under the bag, putting a water purifying tablet into the mug. 'You all just saw what I've done. We will leave that dripping away until after the lesson. The next thing I want to show you is a water vine.' He lifted up off the table what looked like a large stick. He handed it to one of the lads at the end of the line saying, 'Have a good look at this and remember what it looks like, then pass it down the line. These vines are abundant in the hulu, and some grow hundreds of feet in the jungle's canopy. When you find a vine, you reach as high up the vine as possible, cut it, then cut it again a couple of feet off the floor. The water out of the vine normally drips out, but sometimes it runs quite freely, so have your mug ready to catch it, or hold it directly over your mouth. The water from the vine doesn't need purifying, but only drink the water if it tastes sweet. If it tastes bitter and you drink it, you will end up with Rangoon Ring.'

When I got to look at the vine I found it to be quite flexible, and I reckoned I would have no trouble in identifying it should I come across one. After everyone checked the vine over it was handed back to the Gurkha corporal. 'Any questions, lads? No. Right, have a ten-minute smoke break while I sort a bit of stuff out. Don't look at the Millbank bag yet,' he said, as a couple of the lads were walking towards it, 'I'll show you at the end of the lesson.'

Most of us walked a few feet to the edge of the jungle to look at all the different trees and plants and to try and spot any wildlife. This was the closest any of us had been to the Hulu. We'd been told this jungle was one of the densest in the world, albeit one of the smallest. After about ten minutes the Gurkha corporal called us back over to the table where he had been joined by another Gurkha corporal, who we got told was there to assist him. We resumed our positions and sat in a semi-circle round the table. It was a very hot day and we were thankful of the shade the palm trees gave us. We could hear all kinds of noises; it was as though the whole jungle was alive. The bush crickets seemed to be the noisiest of the lot. The Gurkha corporal pulled back a sheet covering the table saying, 'The fruit, insects and plants on this table are just a few of the many foodstuffs in the jungle that will keep you alive. There are far too many to display here. Don't worry if you can't remember what they are or where you can find them – I will give you all a flyer later. This will have pictures of the fruits, plants and insects and how to find them.' The Gurkha corporal lifted a coconut up off the table saying 'the two most common fruits are the coconut and the banana. The other fruits on the table are the durian – very tasty, the mango, papaya, star fruit and water apple. They are all labelled, along with the insects, so you know which is which. As I've said, these are just a few of the many foodstuffs that you can survive on, should you ever need it. Right, lads, stand up and have a look at the kit on the table.'

All the insects were dead and in clear plastic boxes. Looking at some of them, I felt like having a kit check. They were some of the weirdest creatures I'd ever seen. Still, if eating them kept you alive, so be it. As we were looking at the gear on the table, the other Gurkha came round each one of us, handing out the flyers. It took about twenty minutes for all the platoon to see what was on the table, and when we'd finished, the Gurkha sat us all back down in our semi-circle again. He looked at us with a glint in his eye as he took a small box from under the table. 'Right, lads, I want two volunteers,' he said. Kid 'The Sprog' put his hand up right away. How many times have these sprogs got to be told 'never volunteer'? The Gurkha called Kid over, saying, 'Turn round and face the lads. I want one more volunteer, come on.' Kenny, willing to have a go at anything, put his hand up. He got called forward to join the kid.

The Gurkha opened the box and walked along the lads, showing each one of us what was in the box. As I looked in, I nearly puked, as did a few of the other lads. When everyone had looked in the box, the Gurkha went back to where Kenny and Kid were standing. He said, 'I've lightly cooked a little snack for you both. I love volunteers.' He said to Kenny, 'Open your mouth.' Kenny did as told, and the Gurkha put a large, thick grub in his mouth, saying, 'Eat that.' Kenny pretended to chew it, but he just swallowed it so he wouldn't have to taste it. The Gurkha then went to Kid, saying, 'Your turn, open up.' Kid had this horrible look on his face. As soon as he saw what was going to be shoved in his gob – it was a large beetle – it got shoved in his mouth and he got told to chew and swallow it. Kid started to chew, and a crunching noise came out of his gob. After chewing for a couple of seconds, he went green round the gills, retched and puked up; all the section was laughing at his misfortune. The Gurkha told Kenny he'd just eaten the larva of the palm weevil and said to Kid that his delicacy was a cicada – he said it was only a small cicada, some of them had a wing span of eight inches. 'Alright, lads, stand up and one at a time go over and check the mug under the Millbank bag. You will see the water is clear, unlike the muddy water that was put into the bag. So, you see, the Millbank bag does its job.' When we had all checked the water out, the instructor said, 'That's all for now. I want you all back here after lunch, dressed in full jungle kit. I will be showing you how to construct your basha using your Australian lightweight kit. After that, just behind us is a circular track roughly four miles long, through this jungle. I will be taking you around this track to give you a taste of the jungle.' The Gurkha saluted the Rupert, saying, 'That's all for now until after lunch, sir.'

Lunch finished, we were all lined up in a small clearing at the edge of the jungle. All of us had put insect repellent on all the exposed parts of our bodies. One of the lads found out about this insect repellent the hard way: after he applied his repellent, he put his hand down his keks to relieve his itchy bollocks and gave them a good scratch. After a couple of seconds, he gave a scream, dropped his keks, pulled his skiddies down and tipped half a bottle of water over his nuts. 'Ho yea,' said Corporal Tenwell, laughing. 'I should have told you about the repellent ... keep it away from your nuts, it will burn them off.'

'Bit late telling me now,' said Kid. 'Me nuts are killing me.'

'Could be worse,' said the corporal.

'How come?' Kid said, rubbing his goolies.

'Could be me,' the corporal said laughing.

The Gurkha corporal came over to us, saying, 'Stand in a large semi-circle round me, get your Australian lightweight kit out and place it on the ground in front of you.' This done, the Gurkha said, 'Okay, lads, I'm going to show you how to build your basha. As you can see, behind me there are a lot of pre-cut poles and sticks. We use these to save chopping new ones every time we get a new class to teach. You should all have lots of string and your bungees with you. If you didn't have string you could always use vines, but string is more convenient. It's not recommended that you sleep on the jungle floor, there's lots of nasties that crawl round. The jungle comes alive at night and everything is on the hunt for food, and you don't want to be on the menu. You have all got an oblong sheet of reinforced plastic, roughly the size of a stretcher. This, in fact, can be used as a stretcher should the need arise.' The corporal got two poles roughly about eight feet tall and slid them down an opening each side of the plastic sheet. 'There,' said the corporal, 'you now have your bed.' The two poles protruded about a foot out of each end of the plastic sheath. The corporal got four sturdy-looking branches, about five to six feet long. He cut a notch in each branch, roughly in the centre. He then put the notches of each branch together, forming a crosspiece and then strapped them together. He made two cross pieces and then rested the cross pieces at the base of two trees about six feet apart. Picking up his stretcher, he placed each end of the stretcher on the crosspieces. Then he lay on the stretcher, saying, 'There you go, lads, that's your bed and it took me less than ten minutes to construct.' Getting up off the bed, the corporal reached for what was going to be the roof of the basha. It was a large sheet of strong plastic; it had metal rings down the sides and ends of it. The corporal placed string through the metal rings, tying the string about five feet high to each tree above the stretcher, then he pulled the corners of the sheet down and tied them to other trees or small bushes, forming a tent shape. He then took his mosquito net out of his pack. He placed a stick at each end of the net so when he fitted it under the canopy of the basha it formed a nice oblong shape, which hung down and gave plenty of room to keep the mossies at bay. The basha built, the corporal said, 'When your basha is finished, you put your kit on each end of the stretcher where you can tuck your mossie net under. If you don't tuck your net up properly, the mossies will get in and drive you mad all night. Right, lads, split yourselves up into groups of five. Each group need to use only one LWK. You have twenty minutes to build your bashers – go.'

I was quickly learning about this jungle stuff. I really loved it and couldn't wait to get into the real thick jungle. As we were constructing our bashas, the Gurkha Cpl came around each one of our bashas, watching our progress. I saw him smiling at some of our attempts. We finished our bashas, and the corporal and his assistant moved from basha to basha making their assessments.

When they finished, they gathered us all round. He said, 'Well done, lads, not bad for your first attempt. Right, repack all your kit and we will go down the jungle track.' All our kit packed, the instructor said to our Rupert, 'I will lead the way sir, If you will put your platoon in order behind me, about six foot apart in single file. My assistant will bring up the rear.'

'Okay, corporal,' replied the Rupert. 'Corporal Tenwell?'

'Yes, sir?'

'Your section will lead the way behind Corporal Shirisha, Sergeant Jools and myself next, followed by 2 Section and 3 Section.'

'Okay, sir,' Corporal Tenwell replied as he started to organise the platoon in order of march.

The jungle track was fantastic. It gave us a great insight into what the jungle was like. I really took to the wildness of it. We didn't need to use our pangas for cutting; it was a well-worn track and we weren't tactical, so we could all chat to each other as we went along. The track was getting steeper, we were going up the side of a very large hill and I thought, this would be really tough going if we weren't on this track. We had been walking for about half an hour; we were all pissing with sweat, the going was getting harder the farther we walked. The insects and birds we saw were unbelievable, none of us had seen anything like this before. It was like being in a different world. Corporal Tenwell, who was following the instructor, excitedly pointed out a snake he had spotted to our instructor. The Gurkha looked over to where Corporal Tenwell was pointing and said, 'That's a green tree pit viper, very poisonous. Snakes tend to move off if they sense any danger towards them.'

'That's nice to know,' replied Corporal Tenwell.

The noises of the insects were everywhere and in the distance we could hear howling, which I was told were monkeys. We eventually got to the end of the track – it was like a large circular track that brought us back about two hundred yards from where we started. Most of us enjoyed the experience, but a couple of the lads were terrified over some of the strange creatures they saw and didn't like the jungle at all. Over the next week, we were taught all kinds of jungle skills: how to set up base camps – 'harbour up' they called it. How to make flotation packs, using our own kit, to cross rivers, water patrols, tree patrols, the Buddy Buddy system, just to name a few. It was a great learning process for us. The ten days soon flew by, and at the end of our course we all retrieved our rifles from the armoury. We loaded ourselves back on our three-tonners to return to Changi Barracks. I don't know why we brought our rifles; we never used them.

Over the next few months, people were getting sent on all kinds of courses, learning different skills. I got sent on a two-week close quarter combat course, followed by a lead scout course. On my lead scout course, apart from jungle skills, I got taught how to use an American AR-15 Armalite – this is what lead scouts used – and for the rest of my stay in Malaya it would now be my personal weapon.

*

The battalion had only been in Singapore for just over four busy months when we got posted to Malaya. At the end of February 1967, we were posted to Selerang Barracks in Terendac Garrison. The Garrison was not far from the town of Melaka. The garrison consisted of a battalion of Australians, a battalion of New Zealanders and us. The Aussies got sent here to train for Vietnam, poor bastards. There were also all the attachments that kept a garrison going. There was a military hospital, Royal Engineers, RMP (Royal Military Police), RCT, Dental Corps, Army Air Corps, just to name a few. It was a large garrison. We had been in our new posting for roughly five months when the platoon commander called me into his office. 'What does the Rupert want me for now?' I wondered.

I knocked on his door.

'Come in.'

I entered his office and saluted him.

He saluted me back and said, 'I've spoken to Sergeant Jools and Corporals Tenwell, Savage and Hay. I've asked them to recommend a rifleman out of our platoon who, in their opinion, would be good enough to pass an NCO's cadre and would make a good corporal. A couple of them told me you took to the jungle like a second home, and they recommended you to me. There's an NCO's cadre starting next week and it will be a month long. There will be over forty personnel from all companies at the start of the cadre and you will be one of them. I'm recommending that you be made a lance corporal. What do you think, H? Do you think you can do it? Out of the starting forty only half or less will pass. Do you want to be promoted to a lance corporal?'

'Yes sir, thank you,' I said.

'Okay, the platoon sergeant will give you all the details. Good luck, and don't let me down.'

'I won't, sir, and thank you.' I saluted and left his office, a big grin spreading across my face.

*

There were actually thirty-nine personnel on the NCO's

cadre. We were all sitting in a large classroom waiting to be told what we would be doing for the next month. The sergeant major in charge of the course entered the room, and a training corporal, who was already in the classroom, said, 'Sit up.' We all sat to attention.

The sergeant major moved to the front of the classroom and stood behind a lectern, facing us all. 'Right,' said the sergeant major, 'you lot have been recommended to be promoted to lance corporal. Well, I'm telling you now, you don't look like NCO material to me. Any of you who cock up on this cadre for whatever reason will be kicked back to your relevant companies. Do you all understand?'

Silence.

He said, 'Do you all understand?'

'Yes, sir,' we said in unison.

The door to the classroom opened and in walked a full lieutenant and three more full corporals. They walked over and stood behind the sergeant major. The sergeant major said, 'The people standing in front of you will be in charge of the NCO's cadre.' The sergeant major turned to the Rupert, saluted him and said, 'The cadre is yours, sir.'

'Thank you, sergeant major.' The Rupert started by introducing his staff to us. 'I'm Lieutenant Winters, and this is Sergeant Major Bender.'

One of the lads started laughing on hearing the sergeant major's name and put his hand over his mouth to supress his laughter. It was too late.

'You, stand up.' The Rupert pointed at the perpetrator. The lad stood up; he wasn't laughing any more. 'What the fuck you laughing at?'

'Don't know, sir,'

'Don't know? Are you some kind of nutter that doesn't know what he's laughing at?'

'No, sir.'

'Get out the classroom, return to your company, you are off the cadre.'

Now there were thirty-eight left. The whole cadre was silent. The Rupert continued. 'As I was saying, this is Sergeant Major Bender.'

Complete silence.

'And these are Corporals Savage, Williams, Sharp and Darks. We will be in charge of this cadre for the next month. You will do what you are told when you are told. There will be no slacking on my cadre. You are here to work for your promotion. If you are ever late attending any lesson, I don't care how good you think you are, you will get the boot. Do you all understand?'

'Yesss, sir.'

'Eighty per cent of what you get taught over the next month you may already know, but by the time the course ends it will be one hundred per cent. Take over the class, sergeant major.'

'Yes, sir. Thank you, sir.'

The first three days of the course were spent learning how to read a map and how to use a compass. Corporal Savage, who was in charge of us, told us the importance of using a compass. He said, 'The Malaysian jungle is very dense and that, while learning how to read a map is essential, the compass, however, will be your main navigational aid. Reading a map in the jungle can be difficult. A small stream marked on your map may become a river overnight after a good downpour. This could make you think that you are in the wrong location. Times like this is when your map-reading skills come into play. Trust your compass – if you read it properly, you will not get lost. The third week of the course, you – whoever's still on the cadre – will be split up into groups and you will be going into the jungle for four days. Each of you will take turns in navigation. The staff will soon know if you can read your compass or not and if not, you know what will happen when we get back to camp.' Over the next two weeks we were taught how to harbour up (set up camp) in the jungle, and what dangers to look for.

A two- or three-man patrol would be sent round the perimeter of the camp, looking for any rotten trees. These trees could come crashing down through the jungle at their life's end, and you wouldn't want a hundred-foot tree crashing through your camp. Water replenishment patrols, river crossing, flotation kits, the Buddy Buddy system, are all taught. The Buddy Buddy system is very important. You always work in pairs. At the end of the day, when you have built your basha, finished patrols and eaten your evening meal, you both strip off to your boots, drop your keks and take your shirt off. You can check the front of your own body, but your back and arse needs to be checked for anything that may be eating you. If you went to your basha with a couple of bull or tiger leeches on you, you will be in trouble. They could take a pint or more of blood and you wouldn't even feel it. Nearly everyone smoked in those days. If you found a leech on you, you never pulled it off your skin – it could cause ulcers. You lit a cigarette and you burnt the leech on its tail and it would fall off you. You never felt these leeches sucking your blood, horrible bastards. You could also get them off you by tipping a bit of insect repellent on them, but this is a slower process. I preferred the cigarette method. I just wanted the slimy blood-sucking bastards off me as fast as possible.

We were in the third week of our course, and none of us knew how well we were doing. We had been whittled down. There were only twenty-six of us left now. Tomorrow we would be going into the jungle for four days. We were almost at the end of the cadre and I wondered out of the twenty-six of us how many would actually be promoted. I was looking forward to our jungle adventure. Most people had spent days or weeks in the jungle, but this will be my first time overnight because I had always been away on courses when my platoon went into the hulu.

Twenty-six survivors sitting quietly in the classroom, waiting for the instructors to come in to give us our briefing for the four-day exercise. I looked round the classroom; it looked much larger now with all the empty seats. The door of the classroom opened and in came all our instructors, the Rupert leading the way. The Rupert made his way to the lectern and the sergeant major and corporals sat down on chairs facing us.

'Right,' the Rupert started, 'there's twenty-six of you that's made it this far. Let's see how many of you will be promoted after your four-day exercise. You are all going to be split up into three sections. Two sections of nine personnel and one of eight. Myself and Corporal Savage will be in charge of 1 Section. Sergeant Major Bender and Corporal Williams will be in charge of 2 Section, and Corporals Sharp and Dark, 3 Section. When you leave the classroom, check the notice board on the wall – you have already been put in your sections, and you can check which one you are in.'

The Rupert turned around after picking up a pointer

stick off the lectern. He pointed the stick at a map on the wall behind him, saying, 'This is where we will be training for the next four days. As you can see, there's two roads, more like large tracks than roads, running almost parallel with each other for about half a mile before they veer off in different directions. The jungle between these roads is very dense. This,' he pointed to the bottom road, 'is where we will be dropped off. The distance between the bottom road and our destination here,' he said, pointing to the top road, 'is just over twenty-eight miles, twenty-eight miles of hills, streams and thick jungle.' Just over twenty-eight miles, I thought, a piece of piss – we are in the infantry after all. As if reading my mind, the Rupert said, 'I know what you are all thinking – twenty-eight miles in four days, no problem. Well, we'll see. I just hope I don't have to call in a chopper to get any of you out because you can't make the grade. Each of you in turn will be leading your section on a given compass bearing and you had better get it right. You've got a half mile leeway where the roads are closest to each other. You miss this and you could end up being lost and eaten alive. Of course, this won't happen because you will have an NCO with you and if we think you are straying too far off course we will stop you and replace you with another student. Don't fuck your bearings up, have confidence in your compass. Before our two-year tour of Malaya is up, most of you will be taking patrols into one of the thickest jungles in the world. If you can't use a compass, you are no good to us. Do you all understand?'

'Yesss, sir,' we all replied as one.

'Sergeant major, continue with the class,' the Rupert said as he left the room.

'Yes sir, thank you. Okay, you lot, you have all got note books and pencils, so take these notes down if you need to. There will be one hour's starting time between each section. You will be dressed in full jungle kit and 1 Section will leave at 0700 tomorrow morning, 2 Section will leave at 0800 and 3 Section 0900. Each section will be operating separately from each other, but we will keep in touch with our radios. Each section will have a radio operator attached to us, from the signals platoon. These radio operators have already been briefed. You will all carry five days' rations, hexamine cookers with spare fuel tablets. You will also take spare water purifying tablets and Paludrine – remember, you won't get malaria if you take your tablets. You will all carry two water bottles. When we get to our drop-off point, one person from each section will be nominated to do the first leg. He will be given his compass bearing and off we go. We won't be tactical, but we will be putting into practice all what we have been taught. Any questions?'

'No.'

'Right, you are all banned from the NAAFI tonight, and no drinking. Anyone found doing either will get the chop. Class dismissed.'

*

The following morning, we were all lined up in three ranks on the road outside our classroom. We had already drawn our weapons out of the armoury. We all had SLRs and all of us had ten rounds of blank ammunition. I was in one section, the Rupert and Corporal Savage in charge of us. Corporal Savage was one of the best corporals, and I got on with him okay. A couple of times when I was training, he came across to me and gave me a few tips. There were two Land Rovers that would be doing a shuttle run between the three sections parked on the opposite side of the road from us, the two RCT drivers standing next to them.

'Right, 1 Section, get on the Rovers,' the Rupert then said to 2 and 3 Section commanders. 'You can stand down till the Rovers come back. The drivers know where to find you.' We loaded ourselves into the Rovers and off we went. Twenty minutes later, we were debussing at our drop-off point. We all lined up on the side of the track-cum-road, checking our rifles and putting our packs on. There were nine of us in this section. The Rupert gave us a quick inspection and told us the order of march. He picked Titch, one of the lads from B Company; I'd seen him about the battalion but never spoke to him till I met him on this cadre. He was to go on the first leg with the compass. He gave Titch a compass and his compass bearing. He also gave him a map showing him exactly where we were on the map. After a few minutes the Rupert said, 'When you are ready, lead off.'

Titch set his compass and brought it up to his eye. He picked out a massive tree about a hundred yards in front of him on his bearing. Turning to the section, he said, 'Come on, lads, follow me.' While using your compass in the jungle, sometimes you have to send someone in front of you and he walks until you can hardly see him. You direct him left or right to keep him on the right bearing. Then you walk the section up to him and repeat the process. The lead man or scout would, if necessary, cut a path for the rest of the section to follow. Titch was followed by the Rupert, then me, followed by the rest of the section, Corporal Savage bringing up the rear. Titch had been leading for about an hour when the Rupert brought us all to a halt, giving the sign for a ten-minute smoke break. He held his clenched fist into the air then spread his fingers out twice, five–ten minute break. This hand signal got passed down the line and we all took our packs off, some of the lads lighting up. A couple dropped their keks to check nothing was feeding on their bits and pieces. The jungle was a magnificent place; it made us look insignificant. I'd never seen or experienced anything like it. I really enjoyed being out here. It was a challenge to me and I would make sure I would learn how to live and survive in this place, I would take in everything I was taught. The Rupert waved me over to him, saying that I would be leading the second leg. He checked the bearing on his own compass then took Titch's compass and map and handed them to me.

'Check your bearing, H, we will be moving in ten.'

'Okay, sir,' I said as I set my compass.

After ten minutes, I said, 'Mount up, lads, let's go.' I picked a massive tree as Titch had, about a hundred yards in front us on my bearing and headed for it, followed by the Rupert who would, I was sure, keep an eye on me. I had my rifle slung over my shoulder and my panga in my right hand. The jungle was getting denser now, and I would need to do some chopping. I led the way up the side of a large hill that seemed to go on forever, the sweat was streaming out of me, I was having to cut through the foliage now, it was so thick. I was glad when the Rupert brought us to a halt and swopped me over so one of the other lads could take the lead. He never let on if I'd done good or not. I must have been okay, or he would have pulled me up.

Four hours later and deep in the Malay jungle, the Rupert brought us to a halt in a small clearing next to a fast-flowing stream, saying, 'We will have lunch here. We move out in an hour's time.' All the lads came into the clearing and started setting up their hexamine cookers to make a brew or cook whatever they fancied to eat. I found what looked like a large oblong lump of rock covered in foliage. I scraped some foliage off the rock where I could also set up my cooker. I placed my pack next to the rock and rested my rifle against my pack. I opened up my solid fuel cooker and placed my hexamine block in it and lit it up. It took seconds to have a good flame going. I placed my mess tin on the cooker, put water in it then opened a tin of compo soup, stirred it into the water, I added an Oxo cube and a spoonful of curry powder. It wasn't long before the smell of curry was filling the air. I was sitting on the rock enjoying my soup looking at the surrounding jungle. I noticed several pillars of foliage sticking up towards the jungle's canopy. They looked out of place. They were about twenty feet high and several feet wide.

I finished my soup and cleaned my mess tin in the stream, putting my mess tin back in its pouch. I doused my cooker with water from the stream and repacked it putting the empty can in a plastic bag I brought just for that purpose. You always bring your rubbish out of the jungle. After all my kit was repacked, I walked over to one of the fingers of foliage. I cleared a little foliage away to find it was covering a large slab of rock. I cleared more foliage off the rock and found the rock was a pillar with all kinds of strange drawings and etchings on it. I called the Rupert over to show him. The Rupert cleared more stuff off the rock; he looked really excited. He turned round to me saying, 'We are in the ruins of some ancient civilisation long retaken by the jungle.' He took out his map and marked out where we were. He also wrote down the compass bearing we were marching on. I was twenty-one years of age then and didn't know much about ancient civilisations, we never got taught in school about such stuff. Now I thrive for knowledge. Every time we stopped, the radio operator would receive or send sitreps to HQ back at base or to the other two sections which were now in the hulu. Lunch finished, we restarted our trek. We were climbing up the side of a large hill and the going was getting tougher. The sweat was pissing out of me now, but I was determined to finish this course and hopefully earn my promotion.

After two more hours of hard slogging, the Rupert brought us to a halt. It was 1600 hours and the jungle went pitch-black by 1800 hours. You could hold your hand up in front of your face and you'd not be able to see it. 'Okay,' said the Rupert, ' we will be bashering up here for the night. Me and Corporal Savage will basha up in the centre, the rest of you spread out evenly in a circle round us, about ten foot apart. Build your bashas and all report back to me in twenty minutes, that's enough time to get it built.'

For the next twenty minutes we got busy doing as we were told, and when we were finished, we all reported back to the Rupert. He told two of us to collect everyone's empty water bottles and refill them in a nearby stream. Two of us had to cut down vines and tie them about three feet high in a circle round our bivvy area. This was to stop you wandering out into the jungle if you had to get up in the night for a piss. If we were tactical, we would have the vine to hold and walk round the bivvy area to wake up the next stag. If you turned over the rotting vegetation on the jungle floor it glowed faintly in the dark and you could follow this glow at night round the perimeter of your camp. It was a good night aid. Two other lads got sent out round our area looking for any rotten trees that might come crashing down in the middle of the night. After all the patrols reported back, the Rupert gave us a quick brief about how our day was going, he also spoke about the ancient ruins we had been in earlier; he seemed really excited about that. 'Right,' he continued, 'we are not tactical so cook your evening meal, you can chat amongst yourselves about how you think you are doing and coping in the jungle, that's it for now, we will be up at first light.'

We all made our way to our bashas and started cooking our meal. My meal finished, I was just about to pour a little water in my mess tin to clean it when Corporal Savage came over to where I was sitting. He said, 'Hi, H, don't waste your water, just leave your dirty mess tin on the jungle floor and check it out tomorrow.'

'Okay, Corporal, why leave it on the floor?'

'Cos it will be sparkling tomorrow morning, there won't be a scrap of food left on it.'

'Thanks for the tip, corporal.'

'No probs, H. Between you and me, keep going the way you are and there's a good chance you will be promoted.' He smiled at me and said, 'Enjoy your first night in the jungle, it's an experience you will never forget. Good night, H.'

'Good night, corporal.'

Just before I hit the sack, Titch came across to me and said, 'Check my back out, H.' He took his shirt off and dropped his keks.

I said, 'There's nothing on your back. Open your own arse cheeks, I'm going nowhere near that.' He reached behind him and opened his cheeks. 'Nothing there either, Titch. You check me now.' I was also clear of the blood sucking bastards.

I was lying in my basha listening to the cacophony all around me – howling, clicking, screaming, rustling, what an experience. I was just dropping off to sleep when someone let out a terrifying scream: 'Get it off meee, help!'

A couple of torches flicked on and I could hear the Rupert shouting, 'What the fucks up?' We wasn't tactical so torches were allowed to be used. The Rupert shoved his way through the jungle to the screamer's basha and shone his torch inside his mosquito net. I heard him shout at the screamer, 'It's just a moth you scrote. You obviously never checked your net when you got in it. Get yourself sorted out.' The torches went out as everyone settled back down. I thought to myself, I would scream out as well if something crawled across my face in the pitch black.

Waking up the following morning, sunlight streaming through the jungle's canopy, listening to the jungle, it was a different kind of noise during daylight. Birds singing and squawking away. Monkeys howling. The crickets never stop, day or night. I got out my basha and reached out for my mess tin to cook my breakfast. My mess tin was sparkling, Corporal Savage was right. I only had to give it a little rub out and it was ready to use. After breakfast we all repacked our gear, putting any rubbish in our packs. Corporal Savage went round all our basha areas to make sure no rubbish was left behind. The Rupert chose one of the lads for the first leg, gave him his bearing and off we went.

The fourth day of our jungle experience found us

coming out of the jungle at our objective. We had made it. You could see by the looks on all the lads' faces that everyone was relieved. We made our way onto the track and sat down at the side of it. The Rupert told the radio op to call for our transport, saying, 'It should already be along this track somewhere.' He told the rest of us, 'While we are waiting for transport, make yourselves a brew and clean your weapons.' After about thirty minutes, two Land Rovers turned up – they were already on the way to our RV, just like the Rupert said. They came to a halt alongside us. One of the drivers, an RCT lad, came over to our officer and saluted him, saying, 'A three-tonner is on its way for the other two sections, sir.'

'Thank you. Okay, 1 Section, mount up.'

Arriving back at our barracks, we dubussed and lined up on the side of the road. The Rupert said, 'Clean your weapons again and hand them into the armoury. Get yourselves shaved and showered, then sort your kit out. You can then stand down until 0900 hours tomorrow. At that time I want you seated in the classroom, all cleaned up in smart jungle greens. It will be the last day of the cadre and you will learn tomorrow who will be promoted. Dismissed.'

That night we all dagged our kit up, made sure our shirts and keks were well ironed. I was that sure the officer, sergeant major and corporals would be discussing who of us would be promoted tomorrow, how many of the remaining twenty-six would make it, and would I be one of them.

At 0900 hours we were all smartly dressed, sitting in the classroom. All the full corporals in their best kit were sitting down on their chairs, facing us. I looked at the corporals and I caught Corporal Savage's eye, and I could have sworn I saw him give me a slight nod of his head, then turned to talk with Corporal Sharp. What did that gesture mean, I wondered. After about five minutes, Lieutenant Winters and Sergeant Major Bender entered the room.

'Sit up,' ordered Cpl Savage.

We all sat to attention.

'Sit easy,' said the officer as he stood behind the lectern, placing a folder and a large envelope he was carrying onto it. The Sergeant Major sat down facing us. The officer unfolded his folder and then ran his eyes over each and every one of us. I'm sure every one of us was filled with trepidation at the outcome of the cadre. We had all worked hard.

When the officer had finished his observations, he started his spiel. 'Okay, this is the last day of the cadre. Sergeant Major Bender, myself and my corporals have discussed in depth who of you will be promoted. Don't despair if you haven't made it this time.' Fuck me, he does have a heart, I thought. 'Some of you were borderline, and your names will be put forward for the next NCO's cadre. Out of the twenty-six students left in front of me, only fifteen will be promoted. When I call your name, you will come to the lectern. You will receive your lance corporal's chevrons, then return back to your seat. The officer reached into the large envelope and took two chevrons out, saying, 'Step forward, Lance Corporal Woods.' Woody marched forward, came to a halt in front of the lectern and saluted the officer. The Rupert saluted Woodsy and handed him his chevrons, saying, 'Well done, Lance Corporal Woods.'

'Thank you, sir.' Woodsy saluted again, done an about turn and returned to his seat.

'Lance Corporal Leatherbarrow.' Up he marched. That's two, I thought.

Eight more guys went up to collect their chevrons, then ten, two more, twelve now. It looks like I'm not going to make it, I thought. I could have sworn that slight nod I got off Corporal Savage was telling me I had made it. I looked across at Corporal Savage and, again, I got a slight nod off him.

'Lance Corporal Ward.' Up he went.

'Lance Corporal H.'

Fuck me, I made it. I was full of elation. I received my chevrons and sat down again.

'Lance Corporal Crew.' The fifteenth and last. After Lance Corporal Crew sat down, the Rupert reiterated, saying, 'Like I said, those of you that didn't make it this time will have another chance on the next cadre. The fifteen newly promoted lance corporals, stay seated, the remainder of you, collect your kit together and return to your companies.' The lads stood up, all with disappointed looks on their faces and made their way out of the classroom, the last one closing the door behind him. The Rupert continued, 'Well done to everyone. At the end of each cadre we pick what we believe is the best overall student. It was a toss-up between three of you. Step forward, Lance Corporal Hayward.' He marched to the lecturn and saluted the Rupert. The Rupert presented a Gurkha's kukri and sheath with a small silver strip of metal attached to the sheath. We all started clapping. 'Well done, Lance Corporal Hayward. Your name will be engraved on the kukri, along with the date of the cadre.'

'Thank you, sir.'

That was it, cadre over. I was now a lance corporal.

*

My NCO's cadre finished, I returned to my company. It was good to be back. For the next couple of months, we did normal infantry training in and around the camp area. It was Friday 'payday'. A bunch of the lads decided to go for a few beers in a couple of bars just outside our camp so I joined them. It was 2000 hours as we walked down the road leading to the bars. The jungle each side of the road was full of noise being made by the night creatures, and it was a very warm evening, which would make the beers go down easy – too easy. We were all bladdered by 2245 hours, so decided to go back to camp and catch the char wallah for something to eat before he closed his shop. We arrived at the char wallah at 2309, and it was closed. Loopy Larry from 3 Platoon was starving. He banged his fist on the door of the wallah's hut, saying, 'Open up, Adji, we are starving out here.'

'Fuck off, Johnny,' came the reply, 'I'm sleeping, go away.'

'How can you be asleep, soft shite? You're talking to me. Open up.'

'Fuck off, Johnny, I'm not opening up, go on, go away.'

'Come on, lads, let's hit the sack,' I said.

We all made our way to our billets where we just sat around, talking and getting ready for bed, the fans blowing cooling air round the room giving a little respite from the heat outside.

BOOM.

'What the fuck's that?' shouted Kid.

We all ran to look out the windows and doors in the direction of the explosion. We looked across the road at the char wallah's hut just as Adji, the char wallah, came staggering out of his hut. He had smoke coming out of his long beard and he was covered from head to toe in shite. He had flour, eggs, tomato ketchup and all kinds of stuff over him. The door to his hut was hanging on one hinge and some of the lourvres had been blown out of the windows. Adji staggered to a set of steps outside his hut and sat down, holding his head in his hands, smoke still coming out of his beard. We ran across to Adji. 'You all right, mate?' someone shouted. The char wallah was covered in shite and dust and was shocked, but he didn't seem to be hurt. Adji was an old man, he was sixty-five and could have had a heart attack.

All of a sudden four of the guards turned up. 'What the fuck's going on here?' shouted one of them.

'Some twat's blown the char wallah's hut up, by the looks of it,' said Geordie.

Two of the guards gently lifted Adji up, saying, 'Come on, mate, we'll take you to the guard room and get a medic to check you out.' The other two guards checked Adji's hut to make sure it wasn't going to catch fire. That done, they started to question us and took our names, no doubt to give to the sergeant major tomorrow.

The guards left, and I said, 'Looks like some twats put a thunderflash through the louvres of the Wallah's hut. Fuck me, the sergeant major's going to throw a fit when he comes in tomorrow morning. Somebody's head's going to roll.'

'Who the fuck done it?' said Geordie.

'That's a daft question,' said Sheriff. 'Can anybody see Loopy Larry?'

We all looked around and Loopy Larry was nowhere to be seen.

'Let's get back to our billets,' I said. 'We are going to be in the shite tomorrow.'

0700 Saturday morning, the whole company was lined

up on parade. The company sergeant major's name was Wolf. He had served a few years with the SAS and wasn't a man to cross. The company officers and sergeants had been excused this muster parade. Just corporals and riflemen on parade. The sergeant major stood in front of the company and ran his eyes up and down the ranks. 'Right, who blew the fuckin' char wallah up last night?' he yelled.

Complete silence. No one ratted in those days; it wasn't the done thing.

'I said, who blew the fuckin' char wallah up last night?'

Still silence.

'Okay,' continued the sergeant major, 'one of you morons could have given the char wallah a heart attack, he's an old man. I want whoever is responsible to report to my office by 1200 hours today, or I want his name handed to me. You will all be back on parade at 1230 and at that time, I better know who it is. Platoon corporal, take over and have the company back here 1230 hours on the dot.' Everybody knew it was Loopy Larry, but no one actually saw him do it, and he denied any involvement.

Back on parade at 1230, the sergeant major standing in front of us said, 'I don't have the culprit's name, so I'm going to ask you all one last time, who blew the char wallah up?'

Still silence.

'Okay,' continued the sergeant major, 'you are all confined to camp until I find out who did it. This includes the pads. You pads will have to find somewhere to get your heads down at night for as long as this goes on. Every day that goes by, you will be smartly dressed and clean-shaven. I don't give a damn if you pads' shaving kit is at home, sort it. You are all banned from the NAAFI after 1800 hours until further notice. I will have the provost staff spot-checking the NAAFI. Any one of you that gets caught disobeying my orders will end up in front of the old man. Corporal Savage, fall the company out.'

'Yes, sir. A Company, to your right, no officer on parade, fall out.' The sergeant major watched the company fall out and watched several pads walk over and surround Loopy Larry, where a heated discussion took place. The sergeant major was very astute; he knew then that it was Loopy Larry, but he would wait for his confession.

Three days of confinement went by, and it wasn't just the pads having a go at Loopy. A couple of the lads had threatened him also. He was really going to get hurt if he didn't own up. The fourth day at 0730 saw Loopy Larry standing outside the sergeant major's office. We were all watching in our billets to see what was going to happen. Loopy knocked on the sergeant major's door, he entered the office and shut the door behind him. We could hear yelling, then silence. I bet Loopy was shitting himself. After several minutes, two provost staff came running down the road and made their way to the sergeant major's office. One of them knocked on the door and they entered, closing the door behind them. After a couple of minutes, Loopy came doubling out the office.

'Mark time,' yelled the provost full corporal. Loopy marked time.

'Get those knees up, your snivelling piece of shite, left right, left right, forward,' said the provost corporal as he and the lance corporal double-marched Loopy to the nick.

Loopy went in front of the CO and got fourteen days' nick and fourteen days' pay loss. All because he wanted a banjo off the char wallah and couldn't wait till breakfast.

The company returned to normal, and all the pads were allowed to go home to their married quarters. There would be a few happy wives when they got home, the lucky bastards. The char wallah's hut got fixed by us. We had to fix the louvres, re-hang the door and scrub and paint the interior. His hut was in better shape now than it ever had been and smelt better too. He had a brand new fridge, and the QM re-stocked his shelves. I suppose all this was to sweeten Adji up. He must have liked his new looking hut, judging from the smile on his face when he entered it. Anyway, things got back to normal. Adji went about his business, selling his wares.

The months were flying by now and we only had about five months left of our tour before we returned to Blighty. In two weeks' time A Company would be doing a two-week final exercise in the hulu. 1, 2 and 3 Platoons would be operating independently from each other in separate parts of the jungle. As always, I could not wait. Another two weeks' holiday for me.

The platoon had already been trekking through the jungle for three, days and it was tough going. We were all carrying one week's rations in our packs, and the weight was beginning to tell on a few of the lads. We were going to be in there for two weeks, and after seven days, a helicopter would re-supply us with another week's rations. We would have to cut a helipad wide enough for the chopper to land. It was good training for us and the chopper pilots. 3 Section was leading the way, followed by 2 Section then 1 Section bringing up the rear.

A hand signal came down the line telling us to have a ten-minute break. After a couple of minutes, another signal came down for an O Group. Corporal Tenwell made his way up the line, meeting Corporal Hay on the way. They made their way to the front of the platoon, where the platoon commander Second Lieutenant Garry was waiting. The O Group finished, the corporals returned to their sections to give them the brief from the platoon commander.

Corporal Tenwell gathered 1 Platoon around him, saying, 'There's a problem up ahead. We are not tactical, collect all your gear together and follow me.' We all grabbed our gear and followed him for a hundred yards or so until we came to the rest of the platoon.

Lieutenant Garry gathered us all together saying, 'A hundred yards in front of us is something I've read about and been told about, but till now had never seen. There are millions of ants on the march and they are moving right across our bearing. The sight of these ants are unbelievable and very scary. We have got to find a way across these ants. The column of ants is about four feet wide. You could almost step across them, but if you slipped and fell into them, they would be up your nostrils, down your ears, attacking your eyes. They would eat you alive. So you lot take a break, and Corporal Tenwell and myself will do a recce to find the best way to cross the obstacle, come on Corporal Tenwell.'

'Yes, sir.'

After about thirty minutes the lieutenant and Corporal Tenwell returned. 'Gather around again, lads, and I'll tell you what the plan is.' We all gathered around the lieutenant, some of us with very worried looks on our faces. 'The marching ants have soldier ants marching on their flanks, looking for any dangers to the column, so we have to be very wary and quick. We mustn't disturb them in any way. Corporal Tenwell noticed the column of ants vanishing for about thirty feet and then re-appearing again. On closer inspection, we found the ants were marching through a furrow about five feet across and a couple of feet deep. This is where we will cross. Corporal Tenwell and myself cleared a path up to the furrow so you won't trip on anything on your run up – the last thing you want is to fall face-first into the ants. We will all line up close behind each other. We will jump over the ants and keep running for a hundred metres or so. I've checked the map, a hundred metres on the other side of the ants is a stream. We will cross that stream and re-group on the other side. Lance Corporal H and Corporal Tenwell, you two will be a few yards from the ants, one of you each side of the track we made. If anyone trips or falls into the ants, it will be your job to get him out and run like fuck to the stream. Sergeant Jools, you will lead, followed by Corporal Hay, then 1, 2 and 3 Section. Sergeant Jools, after you have jumped across, go forward about twenty feet or so where you feel safe and then watch everyone across. Corporal Hay, you will lead the lads to the stream. When everyone's across, Corporal Tenwell and H will jump. I will be the last man. Right, lads, start lining up in order behind Sergeant Jools.'

As the platoon was lining up, Kid came up to me, he was almost in tears. 'I can't do it, corporal, I'm terrified and my legs are shaking like jelly.'

I put my arms around Kid's shoulders and took him to one side. 'Look, Kid, you're terrified, I'm glad you told me, I thought it was just me. I'm shitting myself and if the truth was known, the whole platoon is shitting themselves, but you are the only one that's voiced it. That tells me deep down you are one of the bravest soldiers here. It takes a brave man to admit fear.' I gave Kid a hug and said, 'Come on, mate, I know you won't let the side down.'

Kid looked at me and said, 'Thanks, corporal, I thought it was just me being scared. I won't let you down, I promise.'

'I know you won't, Kid. Go and join the line.' Kid went and joined the line behind Corporal Hay.

Second Lieutenant Garry, who had been listening to my little chat with Kid, came over to me and said, 'Well done, Corporal H, you handled that well.'

'Thank you, sir.'

'Right, H, go and join Corporal Tenwell at the front of the track.'

As I approached, I could hear the ants before I could see them. It was a loud rustling noise and when I eventually saw them, it was a horrifying sight. Sergeant Jools came up to where we were standing, followed by Corporal Hay and the rest of the platoon. I could see fright etched on some of the lads' faces. I walked over to Kid and gave him a pat on his shoulder. I smiled and said, 'See you on the other side.' He just gave me a nervous smile and said 'Thanks, H.'

Sergeant Jools turned to Corporal Hay, saying, 'Ready, pass it down the line, go.'

Sergeant Jools ran down the cleared path and jumped. He cleared the ants and ran twenty or so feet into the jungle then stopped to watch the lads jumping over the ants. Corporal Hay was second to jump, and he ran past Sergeant Jools, leading the following lads to the safety of the stream, Sergeant Jools ushering them on their way. I watched the ants as all this was going on and they didn't seem to be perturbed; the soldier ants were darting all over the place, looking agitated, but none followed the fleeing squaddies. Almost everyone over, it was my turn. I ran and, as I jumped, I looked down at the ants and, in that split second, I thought there would be no way we would have been able to save anyone should they have fallen amongst those ants. Thud, I landed on the other side and took off, following the tracks the lads had made. I wasn't kidding Kid when I told him I was shitting myself. Corporal Tenwell was across now, followed closely by Lieutenant Garry.

We all made it; it was a sight I would never, ever forget. We all reached the stream and crossed over to the other side, just in case the ants changed direction; they would not have got over this fast-flowing stream. We all stood around chatting and commenting on what we had experienced.

One of the lads said, 'Imagine being asleep in your basha when they swarmed all over you.'

'Fuck me,' piped up Ken, 'you wouldn't have a chance.'

All of a sudden, the jungle didn't seem the place to be anymore, with that thought going through my mind. After about five minutes the platoon commander gathered us around saying, 'Well done lads, that was an experience and a half. Right, we move out in ten minutes, 1 Section leading, followed by 2. 3 Section tail end, Charlie.'

It was the seventh day of the exercise and for the last couple of hours we had been travelling through some really wet terrain. Leech country. I couldn't wait to check myself, although I couldn't see any telltale signals of blood on my shirt or keks. We started a steady climb out of the swamp area to reach higher ground. After trekking uphill for an hour the platoon commander called an O group. The corporals came off the O group and informed their sections what was going on. We were to set up camp here until 1530 hours then we would have another hour's trekking before we settled for the night. Each of the three sections were given tasks to do. It was 1200 then, we would all have lunch, and at 1300 hours get on with our tasks. 1 Section had to cut a helipad. The chopper would be landing at 1500 hours so that would mean two hours of hard graft, cutting trees and clearing scrub. We found an area that didn't have massive trees in it and started our task. The cutting, hacking and sawing went on for an hour and a half and we were all fucked. Still, the helipad was finished with a half hour left to go. We had all finished our tasks, so we broke up into pairs for a Buddy Buddy session, checking each other for leeches and ticks. I paired off with Geordie. I dropped my keks and skiddies and took my shirt off. I felt a warm sensation on my back. I checked the front of my body and found two leeches on my leg. I lit a cigarette and burned the horrible bastards off me. I held the ciggy on the leeches' tails and they fell off me, leaving a small trail of blood.

'You've got two on your back, H.'

'Thanks,' I said, handing Geordie my ciggy. Geordie cleared my back, then I leant forward, pulling my cheeks apart. 'Check my hoop, Geordie,' I said.

After checking my hoop, he said, 'There's nothing up there but shite.'

I had just finished checking Geordie, who was leech-free, when we heard a scream. Curly from 2 Section came staggering over to the platoon commander, holding his keks round his knees. He screamed at the Rupert, 'I've got a leech down my pipe, I've got a leech down my pipe and there's blood coming out of my cock.' The Rupert took one look and screamed for the medic. A couple of seconds later, the medic was looking at Curly's pipe.

'Bloody hell, this is a first,' said the medic. 'I'd better put my marigolds on before I touch that.' The medic reached into his pack and donned his gloves. He then got a pair of tweezers. There was about a quarter of an inch of swelling leech hanging out of Curly's pipe, and his cock was swelling by the second. The medic said, 'If your cock keeps swelling like this, it will keep your wife happy.' Half the platoon was standing round watching the proceedings. 'Stop taking the piss,' whined Curly, 'get it out.'

The medic said to the Rupert, 'I can't pull it out, it could cause an ulcer, so I'm going to cut the leech's tail off, this will stop the leech from sucking any more blood.' The medic got his tweezers and pulled the leech's tail taut. He got a pair of scissors and moved them towards the end of Curly's cock.

The look of horror on Curly's face. 'Be fuckin' careful with those scissors,' Curly whined. The medic cut through the leech's tail, and blood spurted all over the medic's gloves. Curly nearly fainted. The medic turned to the Rupert, saying, 'He will have to be casevaced on the chopper and taken straight to the garrison hospital. I will put a sterile dressing on him in the meantime.' Since the medic cut the leech, the swelling had started to subside in Curly's cock. I saw a look of relief on Curly's face as the medic began to patch him up.

There was a scurry of activity when we could hear the chopper approaching. 'Right,' said the Rupert, Corporal Stone, 'put some smoke down for the chopper. Lance Corporal Ellis, you marshal it down.'

'Right sir.'

'When the chopper lands, Corporal Hay and Stone unload the rations. When the rations are unloaded, Sergeant Jools, you get Curly, his pack and rifle on the chopper.'

'Right sir.'

'Corporal H and Corporal Bar, you two put any rubbish on the chopper.'

'Okay, sir.'

The chopper came into view and started to descend through the jungle's canopy. Lance Corporal Ellis was doing a good job marshalling. The chopper's rotors were skimming the edge of the jungle and blowing leaves and shite all across the camp area. The chopper pilot's skill was something to see; he landed his craft perfectly. The chopper pilot had already been told he'd got a casevac so he kept his rotors turning when he landed. It went like clockwork, the loading and unloading of our rations, getting Curly and the rubbish on board took less than ten minutes and the chopper was on its way with a very worried casualty. A few minutes after Curly came to the platoon commander with his problem, there wasn't one soldier that didn't have his keks down checking his bell end, including the sergeant major and Rupert.

We had all been supplied with one more week's rations each. We packed our gear and struck camp as the Rupert said we could get another hour's trekking in before we harbour up for the night. 1 Section led the way, with me up as lead scout. The platoon had been slowly climbing up this large hill and the jungle here was very dense. Most of these hills had small tracks running along their ridges, caused by many animals and forest people, although I had never come across any people on my jungle travels. Reaching the top of the hill, I came across one of these tracks, which made the going easier. The track just happened to be going in the direction we were travelling. The Rupert called a halt for a small break. Lieutenant Garry called me and Ken over, saying, 'Go and do a quick recce up the track to see if it continues on in our direction. Ken and I had been walking for ten minutes when I told Ken to carry on as I needed a piss and I would catch him up. 'Just stay on the track,' I told him. After a couple of minutes Kenny came running back down the track and ran straight past me. 'Fucking stop!' I shouted. 'What's the matter with you, and where is your pack and rifle?'

Kenny stopped and came back to me saying 'I dropped my pack and rifle on the track because a fuckin' big snake was about to attack me.'

'Fuck off, Ken, we have got to go back and get your weapon and pack.'

'I'm not kidding, H, I've only seen a couple of snakes, but this one is a monster compared.'

'We've still got to get your weapon, come on.'

'You lead, H.'

'Okay, let's go.'

We slowly and carefully edged our way towards where Kenny said he saw the snake. I turned around a small bend in the track and spotted Ken's rifle and pack lying on the track. I raised my eyes, and about fifty feet beyond the pack, I saw it. It was the biggest snake I had ever seen. There were about three coils of snake with the rest of the body standing about three feet above the coils. As I came to a halt, Kenny almost bumping into me, we both looked at the snake as it reared backwards and hoods appeared each side of its head as if it was about to strike. I pulled the quick release on my pack and it dropped to the floor. I managed to keep a hold of my ArmaLite as I turned and screamed at Kenny, 'Fuckin' run!' We ran down the track and didn't stop till we got back to the platoon.

'What's the matter,' yelled the Rupert, 'and where is your fuckin' weapon?' I explained to the Rupert what had happened and told him the rifle is on the track and was not lost. I suggested to wait a while and try again. Hopefully the king cobra would have gone by then. 'Okay, H, we will give it ten minutes and we'll have to go. We will be harbouring up in thirty minutes.'

'OK sir, and the track is going in our direction, by the looks of it.'

I led the way back up the track followed by the Rupert, then Ken, then the rest of the platoon. The Rupert had his SLR cocked ready to shoot at the snake should the need arise. Even if he missed, hopefully the bang would scare it off. 'It's just round this small bend, sir,' I said.

The Rupert lifted the rifle into the aim, telling me to get behind him. We slowly crept forward; we could see both our packs and Kenny's weapon 'Where's the snake, H?' whispered the Rupert.

I looked towards where I saw it and it was gone. 'Looks like its fucked off, sir,' I said.

'Right, retrieve your rifle and packs. You H, will resume lead scout.'

'Okay, sir.' I put my pack on and started along the ridge followed by Corporal Tenwell and the rest of the platoon. Corporal Tenwell couldn't help having a dig at me and Kenny and suggested we were talking bullshit and no king cobra was as big as we said it was. I didn't like Corporal Tenwell, but I had to admit he was a fit fucker, carrying all that kit on his back.

We started to descend down the hill. I was still in the lead when I got caught up in some Wait-a-while vines. If this happens, you stay still and gently lift the vine off you and let it go. Wait-a-while is aptly named; I don't know what its real name is, but it's a very strong vine with razor-sharp thorns all over it. The thorns face up the vine. It's a vicious plant and if you tried to barge your way through it, it would rip you apart. Hence the name Wait-a -while. Anyway, I lifted the vine off me and continued cutting my way through the bush. It was just after 1600 hours when we got the order to harbour up for the night. It had been a long, hard day full of incidents and we were all goosed and looking forward to a good night's sleep. Harbour area set up, bashas built and a full belly, I was lying in my basha listening to the sounds of the jungle, feeling very content. I closed my eyes and slept.

Rising the next morning, I checked my boots out, gave them a good bang against a tree to make sure I never had any unwanted lodgers. I got a clean pair of socks and put a little foot powder in each one. Socks on, boots on, I reached under my basha for my mess tin, which was sparkling clean, not a scrap of food to be seen. It was a good tip the corporal of my NCO's cadre gave me. I rinsed my mess tin out and prepared my breakfast. One more week to go. We struck camp with 3 Section leading the way.

We had been trekking for a good three hours when we

came up to a clearing by the side of a river. The river was about twenty feet across and looked inviting for a swim. Lieutenant Garry took off his pack, put it down and laid his rifle on top of the pack. He cut a staff about six feet long of a nearby tree. He then entered the river, prodding the stick in front of him, checking the depth. The water was only waist-high. He came back out of the river saying, 'Strip off, lads, go and have a swim. We'll have an hour's break here, so brew up if you want.'

Most of the lads stripped naked and ran into the river; some lads started to cook their lunch. I rested my rifle on my pack, stripped off and ran into the river to join the rest of the lads. This was a good area for a break. All the lads were having a good time, splashing around and dunking each other in the cooling water. All of a sudden, Lieutenant Garry gave a scream and came splashing out of the water. He looked down at his helmet to see a small terrapin hanging from his foreskin. He squeezed the terrapin's head till it let go and then launched the terrapin into the hulu. Before he could tell everyone to get out the water, it was already done. When the lads heard the Rupert scream and saw the terrapin hanging from the Rupert's helmet they were only seconds behind him getting out the water. The Rupert recovered his composure and said, 'If anyone wants to go back in the water, put some keks on.' Lieutenant Garry checked his helmet, and he only had a small nick. He got some antiseptic cream off the medic and applied it to his wounded foreskin. It's a good job it was only a small terrapin. Now I knew why everybody calls the Rupert 'Clit Dick'.

Only four days left of the exercise now and we were making our way round the side of a very steep hill. To the right of us was a deep gully, which made the going hard and dangerous. It was scary looking down that gully. Corporal Tenwell was about ten metres in front of me, barging his way through the bush, as was his way. All of a sudden I saw his arms flailing in the air, he lowered his head like a bull charging and pushed his way through the bushy entanglement in front of him. Then, it was unbelievable: I saw Corporal Tenwell swing right across the gully. It looked like he was just swinging in the thin air. I rushed forward and there he was, swinging and dangling about thirty feet above the gully. There was one vine of Wait-a-while wrapped around his pack stopping him from falling. He stopped swinging and just hung there with a look of horror on his face. 'Get me the fuck down!' he screamed.

I burst out laughing; I knew he was in a dangerous predicament, but I just couldn't stop myself.

Ken came rushing up beside me, took in the situation and said, 'How the fuck we going to get him down?'

'Go up the file, tell the Rupert what's happened and on your way back, collect half a dozen toddle ropes off the lads,' I said.

'Okay, H, be back in a minute.'

I looked across at Corporal Tenwell. Still tittering, I said, 'You are being kept aloft by a single vine of Wait-a while, so keep still. I know it's strong stuff, but you are carrying a lot of weight. I saw what happened, it's your own fault. You got tangled up in the vine and thought you could barge your way through it. It whipped you off the side of the hill, and that's why you are in this mess.'

'Stop your fuckin' lecture and get me down, you moron,' replied Corporal Tenwell.

The Rupert turned up. 'Bloody hell, how we going to get him down?'

Just then, Ken turned up, accompanied by Geordie. They had half a dozen toddle ropes with them.

I said, 'Attach the ropes together and we will use it to get Corporal Tenwell back.'

'Good thinking, H,' said the Rupert. Corporal Tenwell was dangling about twelve feet away from us.

I said to Geordie, 'Hold the end of the rope, you are a strong lad. I'm going to throw the rope to the corporal and when he gets hold of it, you and Ken start slowly hauling him in. Sir, you and I will get ready to grab him when he becomes in reach, is that okay, sir?'

'Okay, H, get on with it.'

'Okay, Corporal Tenwell, get ready to catch the rope and keep a bloody good grip on it.'

I propped myself behind a small tree so I wouldn't slide down the gully and I threw the rope. He missed grabbing it and, as he reached for the rope, the vine slipped its grip and Corporal Tenwell let out a scream as he fell a couple of feet. It looked like the vine was going to release its burden.

'Throw it again,' yelled Corporal Tenwell, a pleading scared look on his face. I readied the rope and threw it again, this time the corporal managed to grab it.

'Hold it firm. Geordie, Ken, start pulling slowly.' They hauled the corporal towards the side of the hill, the vine stretching to allow us to do this. The corporal was only a couple of feet from us when the Rupert and myself managed to grab him. We pulled him onto the side of the hill and I cut the vine off his pack with my panga.

Corporal Tenwell scrambled to safety on the side of the hill. He propped his back against a tree. He was shaking like a leaf. He looked at us with a thankful look on his face and said, 'Thank you, sir, thank you lads.' He looked at me and said 'Thanks, H.'

'No problem, corporal, sorry for laughing.'

The Rupert said to Kenny, 'Return the toddle ropes to the lads, we will move out in ten minutes.'

In our ten-minute break all the lads had heard about Corporal Tenwell's mishap and were amused at the story. Most of them thought it couldn't have happened to a better man. Corporal Tenwell wasn't in everyone's good books.

*

A couple of days of our exercise left now, and we were on the move. 1 Section was in the lead, and I was lead scout followed by Corporal Tenwell. I wondered if that episode of Corporal Tenwell hanging over the cliff would mellow him out. No chance; he was stuck in his disciplinarian ways.

I was about forty feet in front of the corporal, hacking a path through the bush, when I came to this massive tree. The roots of this tree weren't round – they were like thick slats. Some of the roots started high up the side of the tree and angled down to the jungle floor. I approached one slanting root about three feet high. I put my left hand on the root and vaulted over it. I vanished below several feet of stinking water that nestled between two roots of the tree. I came up out of the water, gasping and cursing. I threw my rifle over the lip of the hole holding the water and just managed to haul myself out. I stood up, feeling like a drowned rat, I grabbed my rifle and looked back down the track to where Corporal Tenwell was fast approaching. I turned back round and rushed forward a couple of yards and hid behind a tree, watching Corporal Tenwell following my track. I could hardly stop myself from laughing in anticipation of what I hoped was to follow. I was not disappointed. Corporal Tenwell put his left hand on the same root as I had. He hopped over the root and vanished below the water. I howled with laughter and ran over to the water hole. Corporal Tenwell's hat was floating on the water, bubbles were coming up and two hands were clawing the air. After a couple of seconds, my laughter subsided. 'Fuck me, he's drowning.' I released my pack, laid my rifle across it and reached into the water shouting for help at the same time. I managed to grab Corporal Tenwell's pack, and it took me all my strength to lift him. As I pulled his head above the water, his eyes were bulging and his lips pursed, sucking in the welcome air. I couldn't hold him, back under he went just as Geordie and Kenny arrived. We all reached into the water and, between us, we managed to pull him out. Luckily, his rifle was jammed behind his pack and not lying at the bottom of the pool. He crawled forward a couple of feet, coughing and spewing water, snot dripping out his nose. He looked a right state.

He rolled over and propped his back against a tree. After a couple of minutes of coughing the shit out of his lungs, he looked at me and said, 'Why are you soaking from head to toe and these two aren't?'

I said, 'I fell in the same hole as you.'

He gave me the evil eye and said, 'Why the fuck didn't you warn me, H?'

'How the hell did I know you was going to fall in the water, corporal? And if you wasn't carrying all that unnecessary kit, you would have been able to get out like I did.'

He looked at me with hatred in his eyes and said, 'I don't like you, H. You had better watch your back.'

'You threatening me in front of witnesses, corporal?'

'Just warning you, you moron,' he growled. He stood up and said, 'Get moving.'

'Okay, Corporal.' I picked my gear up, donned my pack and resumed my position as lead scout.

The rest of the day went by with no more incidents to talk about. However, on more than one occasion, I caught Corporal Tenwell giving me the evil eye. If he was a more amicable corporal I would have warned him about the water hole. I thought, I'm going to have to keep my wits about me, he'll be after me now. After a couple more hours' trekking, we harboured up for the night.

The next day was our last full day in the jungle. It was early morning and the jungle was full of life. The birds singing and squawking, the bush crickets clicking and monkeys howling in the distance. The platoon commander gathered us all together for a brief. 'Right, lads, it's almost the end of the exercise. This morning we will trek to within a half-mile of where we will be getting picked up by the transport to take us back to camp. It should take us about two hours. We will then harbour up for the night. As you know, the last night in the hulu we have a bit of a sing-song round a campfire. General admin and such, shave all that two weeks' growth off your face – Kid, you hang your chin in the breeze, it will get rid of that fuzz.' A few of the lads laughed at Kid's expense. 'Corporal Tenwell, after all the shite you've been through, your section will be third in line.'

'Okay, sir.'

'Order of march, 3 Section, 2 and 1. Corporal Stone? Get your section ready. We will be moving out in five minutes.'

'Okay, sir.'

Two hours of hard trekking brought us roughly a half-mile from where we would eventually get picked up by our transport. Corporal Stone found a bit of a clearing in the jungle by the side of a small stream. He called the platoon commander forward, saying, 'This clearing would be a good place to spend our last night in the hulu.' The platoon commander agreed and told Sergeant Jools to gather the platoon together for a chat.

We all sat down in the clearing, some lads lighting up ciggies and others checking for leeches and ticks. The Rupert said, '2 Section, the chopper will be landing at 1400 hours. It's 1030 now, so you will have plenty of time to cut the helipad. Corporal Hay? I will leave you to organise that.'

'Yes, sir.'

'We will all muck in together,' continued the Rupert. 'Clear an area for the fire, build your bashas in a circle around the fire area. I'll leave you all to get on with it.'

Bashers built, helipad sorted, the camp was a hive of activity. A perimeter vine encircled the camp so no one would go astray in the night. Water replenished, tree patrols finished, Buddy Buddy system all done. A few of the lads had ticks and a couple of god-knows-whats eating away at their skin, and a few leeches got the ciggy treatment. We wouldn't light the fire until the chopper had come and gone; it would blow it all over the jungle. All the lads were busy shaving, getting into dry kit, sorting their feet out. We always kept a clean set of kit, shirt, trousers, skiddies and socks for our last day in the jungle.

We all removed our jungle hats as we watched the chopper slowly descend through the jungle canopy. The helipad was cut a fair distance from our bivvy area – we didn't want the chopper to blow our camp all over the place. The chopper landed and the pilot shut his engine down, the 'thwok, thwok' noise of the spinning rotors coming to an end. The pilot and his navigator stepped out of the chopper and walked over to where we were standing.

Our Rupert greeted them. The chopper crew removed their helmets. 'God, it's hot with these bone domes on,' one of the pilots said. The pilot extended his hand to our platoon commander and shook hands. After a few exchanges of pleasantries, the pilot said, 'Curly got his cock sorted out in the garrison hospital. They got the leech out of his pipe and he's right as rain now.'

'Good news,' said the Rupert. 'I bet the poor man was terrified.'

The pilot said, 'Can you get a couple of your lads to put any rubbish securely on the chopper? And also there are a few crates of beer, enough for two cans each.'

Grins spread across the lads' faces as they heard this news. The last night in the jungle after a two-week exercise, it was the norm to have two beers each. I suppose the thinking behind this was so all the lads, when they got back to camp, don't run amok down town pissed out their heads.

After the chopper left, we all started cooking what was left of our rations. Everything got put in a mess tin and most of the lads added heaps of curry powder to the concoction. It wasn't long before the smell of curry wafted round the bivvy area, getting our tastebuds going.

After our lunch, some of the lads started collecting firewood, others shaving and generally getting kit sorted, ready to move out the hulu tomorrow. I was sitting down on a log, finishing my curry off and hoping I didn't end up with Bombay Butt in the morning, when I saw Geordie start to cut down a tree just outside our basha area. Curry finished I stood up and walked over to Geordie and asked, 'Why are you cutting down that tree? This tree will keep us going all night, there's loads of wood already cut over by the helipad. There's no need to cut this tree down.'

'Sorry, corporal, I wasn't thinking. Anyway, I'm half way through now so I might as well finish the job off.'

The tree was tall and slender, about a foot across and thirty feet high. It was just on the camp's perimeter. There was a large V-shape cut in the tree trunk, facing away from the camp, where Geordie was cutting it.

I said, 'you had better stop cutting that tree, Geordie, it's going to fall right through the middle of our camp.'

'No, it's not,' replied Geordie. 'The tree will fall into the V I'm cutting out.'

'It falls away from the V, idiot, you are going to wreck our camp.'

'No, it doesn't, it falls into the V – that's why I've cut the V facing away from the camp.'

Fuck me, he's got more brawn than brains, I thought. 'Right.' I folded my arms and watched Geordie as he continued to happily hack away at the tree. After a few more chops there was a loud creaking noise. The tree was getting ready to fall. Geordie stood back and looked smugly at the tree. Another loud creak and the tree leaned slightly away from the large V cut in its trunk. The look of horror on Geordie's face as he realised the tree was going to fall away from the V and it was going to crash right through our camp.

'Fuckin' hell!' he yelled. He put both his hands on the tree trunk and tried to hold it up.

'The fucking idiot.' I ran into the camp screaming, 'Clear the camp, clear the camp, a tree is going to crash through us!'

The lads started to run in all directions away from the camp area. There was another loud crack and Geordie just about managed to jump out of the way of the falling tree. All the lads managed to clear the camp area as the tree started to fall towards it. The platoon commander was sitting on a log outside his basha eating the last of his rations. He had a mess tin of steaming hot curry and was getting ready to enjoy it when the tree came crashing towards him. He was the last to react to the situation. He screamed as he jumped to his feet; he screamed even louder as his hot curry fell into his groin area. Still screaming, he just managed to get out of the way of the falling tree. The tree came to rest right on top of the Rupert's basha. It was the only basha that got destroyed, the branches of the tree missing all of the other bashas.

The lads, realising no one was hurt, started laughing.

'Shut the fuck up,' yelled the Rupert. 'What moron cut that fucking tree down?'

Poor Geordie walked sheepishly into the camp area. 'It was me, Sir.'

'You fuckin' imbecile, you've roasted my nuts and nearly killed me with that fucking tree, bleeding moron. Get that tree sorted out, rebuild my basha and make me another curry, get on with it.' The Rupert brushed the now cooling curry away from his groin area, he dropped his keks and skiddies and started to check his tackle. A couple of us were watching the Rupert, a look of pain on his face. His groin area was all red, and it did look painful. The Rupert looked across at poor Geordie as he was going about his tasks. 'You fuckin' moron,' the Rupert repeated as he went about rubbing cream on his scalded bits.

Geordie looked like a little kid who had just been told off as he went about his chores sorting the Rupert's basha out. Half a dozen of the lads chipped in to give Geordie a hand, and it wasn't long before they cleared the tree away and rebuilt the Rupert's basha. Geordie managed to scrounge some spare food off the lads to make the Rupert his curry.

The tree had been removed and chopped up ready for the fire, everyone had shaved, eaten, flannelled themselves down in the nearby stream, checked themselves out and done the Buddy Buddy system. We all put on clean shirts, keks and socks. Everyone was feeling good except for the platoon commander, who kept rubbing his groin area and now and then, glaring at Geordie as though he wanted to throttle him. We all placed logs around the fire area just outside our bashas, where we could all sit when the fire got lit.

It was 1700 hours when the whole platoon was sitting around the fire the Rupert had just set alight. It wasn't a large fire, but we had enough firewood to last us a week, thanks to Geordie. Everyone seemed to be having a good time chatting and telling jokes. Sergeant Jools was sitting opposite me, he had the crates of beer by the side of the log he was sitting on. He called over Corporals Tenwell and Hay, he handed the beer to them, saying, 'Give all the lads two beers each.'

I knew Beaver, a lad from 2 Section who didn't drink, and I scrounged his beers off him. He said he would sneak them to me after he received them. Corporal

Tenwell got to me and before he gave me my two beers he shook the cans for a good minute. He then handed them to me saying, 'Hope you enjoy them, H.' He had an evil glint in his eyes.

'Thank you, corporal, that's just the way I like my ale.'

He just grinned at me and moved on down the line.

A few minutes later, Beaver sneaked his two beers to me. 'Thanks, mate,' I said. I gave one of the shaken beers to Ken and I kept the other one. It would take a while before they would settle down. I cracked a can of beer I got off Beaver and took a sip out the can. It was warm, but good.

Ken opened his can, saying, 'Cheers mate, that Corporal Tenwell is a right prat.'

'You're right there, mate, that's why I nearly drowned the bastard between the roots of that tree.' We both broke out laughing.

The night was going well, everyone was having a great time and even the Rupert seemed to be getting over his roasted nuts as he joined in the singing and telling of jokes. I noticed Geordie was sitting as far away from the Rupert as he could; he wasn't that thick, after all. Wise move, I thought. The fire started to die down a little, so I stood up and went over to the pile of logs. I lifted a log up and, to my horror, a scorpion fell off the log onto my arm. The scorpion started to walk up my arm towards my rolled up shirt sleeve. I thought 'Fuckin' hell, I don't want that to crawl under my sleeve.' Trying to keep calm, I turned to the platoon sergeant and said, 'I've got a scorpion on my arm' as I reached for a leaf off a nearby bush. Snapping the leaf off the bush, I placed it in front of the scorpion walking up my arm.

'Keep calm, H,' said the platoon sergeant. The

scorpion reached the leaf, touched it with his pincers then turned round and started walking back down my arm. The sweat was dripping off my forehead. I knew that little scorpions were the most dangerous. The platoon sergeant, who was sitting on a log just in front of me, said again, 'Keep calm, just carry on putting the leaf in front of it. When it walks on the leaf, throw it on the fire or stamp on it.'

All the lads were gathering around to get a look at what was going on. The scorpion reached the leaf once more, and again it turned away from the leaf. It wasn't working, and I was shitting myself. I drew in a big, deep breath and I blew at the scorpion. It flew off my arm and landed on Sergeant Jools' chest. He let out a loud blood-curdling scream, jumped up and shook the scorpion off his shirt. The scorpion went flying into the fire.

'You stupid prat, it could have killed me!' he screamed.

'Sorry, serge, I didn't know what else to do.'

So much for keeping calm, I thought. I felt like laughing, but thought better of it.

Show over, everyone resumed their chatting and singing and as the hours went by. One by one, the lads made their way to their bashas. Eventually there was only four of us left sitting next to the fire. Sergeant Jools stood up, saying, 'When you three are ready for kip, make sure you put the fire out properly.'

'Okay, sergeant.'

Ten minutes after the sergeant's departure we got up ourselves and put the fire out, using water from the stream. We made our way to our bashas using our torches as it was pitch black after the fire was out. This would be my last night in the jungle.

The following morning, most of the lads were cooking what was left of their rations and sorting their kit out. Breakfast over, Corporal Tenwell came round the camp area checking for rubbish giving me the evil eye as he passed. Sergeant Jools came over, saying, 'We move out in twenty minutes. Corporal Hay, your section will lead, Corporal Stone will be next, followed by Corporal Tenwell. Start sorting your sections out.'

Twenty minutes later, we moved out, Corporal Hay's lead scout, Erik, leading the way. Half an hour's trekking saw us coming out of the jungle onto the track, where we would eventually get picked up. Sergeant Jools lined us all up along the track, facing back into the jungle. He gave the order 'For Inspection Port Arms.' We pulled the working parts of our weapons back so the Rupert could make sure none of us had a blank up the spout. The Rupert walked down the ranks, checking each weapon, and gave the order 'Ease Springs' as he did so. All our pyrotechnics and blank ammo was handed in to Sergeant Jools. As each of us handed in our blanks and pyrotechnics, we all made the declaration 'I have no blank rounds or pyrotechnics in my possession, sir.'

We were only about twenty minutes out of the jungle when our transport arrived, the two three-tonners coming to a halt just in front of us. The two drivers switched off their engines, got out their cabs and made their way to the back of the trucks, where they dropped the tailgates in preparation for us to embus. They saluted our Rupert, who returned the compliment, saying, 'Thanks, drivers, you are spot on time.' He then turned to the platoon and gave the order to mount up.

That's it, our last taste of the jungle on that tour. Arriving back at the garrison, the three-tonners dropped us off outside our billets. We all lined up in ranks of three on the side of the road. Sergeant Jools brought us to attention for the Rupert. Lieutenant Garry stood in front of the platoon; 'Stand at ease,' he ordered. The platoon stood at ease. 'Stand easy.' The platoon relaxed. 'Okay, lads, that's our last exercise finished. Everything went well apart from a few mishaps.' He looked across at Corporal Tenwell with a wry smile on his face. 'When you get fell out from here, you will go to your billets, you will strip and clean your weapons and lay them on your beds for inspection. Platoon corporals will inspect them in exactly one hour's time. After the inspection you will hand your weapons into the armoury. The rest of the day will be personal admin. For the pads, a bus will be leaving from the drill square at 1700 hours to take you to your married quarters. That's it for now. Sergeant Jools, take over the platoon.'

'Yes sir.' Sgt Jools turned to face the platoon. 'Stand ready,' he ordered. 'To your right, to your duties, officer on parade, fall out.' The platoon snapped to attention, turned to the right, saluted, marched forward three paces and broke ranks.

Only a couple of months left of our tour now and although I loved it out here I was looking forward to getting back to Good Old Blighty. The battalion was getting really busy now getting prepared for our return to the UK. Packing, cleaning, scrubbing, everything had to be spotless for the battalion taking over from us.

It was our last week, and our platoon, along with the rest of the company, were getting all our Far Eastern kit together to hand back into the colour sergeant's stores. Our platoon was first to hand back our kit. We were lined up in front of the colour sergeant, who was sitting behind a trestle table with a big ledger in front of him. We were in a small clearing behind the colour sergeant's stores. Behind the colour sergeant were half a dozen storemen ready to do his bidding. A couple of these storemen were busy building a fire on the clearing, about twenty metres behind the colour sergeant's table. I wondered what the fire was for. I was soon to find out.

The colour sergeant called the first soldier in line to his table saying, 'Name?'

The soldier (Kid) told him his name.

'Right, hand your kit over to me as I call the items out. Three shirts.'

Kid reached into his rucksack and pulled out his three shirts, putting them on the colour sergeant's table.

'Two pair jungle boots, three shorts.'

Each time the colour sergeant called out an item, Kid put it on the table.

'Two water bottles and two mugs.'

'Sorry, sergeant, I have only got one water bottle and mug.'

'Okay, sign next to your name in the ledger and the price of a water bottle and mug will be docked out of your pay.'

The kid signed and handed over the rest of his kit. The only thing the kid was deficient of was his water bottle and mug. A couple of the storemen came over to the table and gathered all Kid's kit together in their arms. They walked over to the fire and turfed all kids kit into the flames. Fuckin' horrible bald headed bastard, I thought. Fancy making the kid pay for his water bottle and mug when they were getting burnt anyway. One by one the platoon went forward, handing in their kit, and at least half the platoon had to pay for one thing or another.

We had all handed in our kit when the colour sergeant and his staff had a thirty-minute break before continuing with the next platoon. A few of us were sitting in our billets just chatting when Geordie piped up, 'That bald-headed bastard made me pay for two shirts, a pair of keks and a water bottle and mug. That's almost a half-week's pay for me and the twat's burning it. What's his problem?'

'Yeh,' said Ken, 'the bastard's way out of order.'

We watched 2 and 3 Platoons handing their kit in and by the looks on some of the lads faces the colour sergeant was giving them the same treatment as we got.

A few of us were sitting on our beds reading and relaxing when Loopy Larry and Henry from 2 Platoon came into our billet. Loopy said, 'Did that bastard charge any of you lot for deficient kit?'

'Yeh,' a few of us replied.

'Half of my kit had been nicked,' said Loopy, 'and I've almost had to pay a full week's wages to that shithouse only to see all my remaining kit thrown on the fucking fire.'

'He's done the whole company and made a few enemies along the way,' said Ken.

'Well, the bastard will regret ripping me off,' said Loopy.

Something told me Loopy would be hatching something up very unpleasant for the colour boy.

None of us had much to do now until we left Malaya. The next few days would be just lazing around. The next day I was looking out the window when I noticed Loopy Larry leaning out of his window in the next block down from ours. He was clocking the colour sergeant's stores. Most of the lads had gone to the NAAFI or for a walk outside the garrison to the small village just down the road. We were all stood down now, our tour almost at an end. There were only a few lads hanging around the billets. I thought I would keep an eye on Loopy to see what he was up to. I didn't have long to wait. The colour sergeant, who was still wearing uniform because he's on the rear party, came out of his stores, turned right up a path that led to HQ Company. The colour sergeant went to HQ Company half a dozen times a day, and Loopy must have known this. On the right of the track about halfway to HQ was a small patch of brush and trees with a big, dead, hollow tree sticking a few feet above the brush. Loopy waited for the colour sergeant to go into the HQ block, about two hundred feet past the patch of scrub. Then I saw him run across the road up the same path the colour sergeant took. Loopy was carrying a pickaxe in his hand. Fuck me, he's going to brain the colour sergeant, I thought. Loopy got to the scrub and vanished amongst the foliage. I was intrigued. I pulled my bed next to the window where I could sit in comfort while I watched what Loopy was up to. After about ten minutes I saw the colour sergeant come out of the HQ building and start walking back in the direction of his stores. As he got level with the scrub, I thought I heard what sounded like a couple of dull thuds.

Whoosh, a swarm of angry wasps came flying out the top of the dead tree stump. The colour sergeant was right in their path, and they attacked him. He gave out a scream and started to run towards his stores. He took his beret off and started to swing it at the angry stinging wasps. Still screaming, he managed to make it to his stores. He whipped open the door, ran in and closed it behind him. A few wasps got into the stores and continued stinging the colour sergeant. The remaining wasps hung around for a few minutes before returning to their hive. As soon as the wasps swarmed after the colour sergeant, I saw Loopy make good his escape. He came out the scrub and made his way in the opposite direction of the colour sergeant, leaving the pickaxe at the scene of the crime.

I looked across at the colour sergeant's store and thought I better check to see if he was alright. I approached his store with caution. As I got to the door, I could hear whimpering on the other side. 'You alright, colour?' I shouted. 'I saw the wasps and they have all gone now. Do you need a medic?' He opened his door and looked at me. I didn't know whether to feel sorry for the bastard or laugh. I thought I would feel sorry for now and leave the laughter till later. He had half a dozen stings on his bald head, already swelling up and turning red. He had stings to his face and hands, and he had lips like a duck-billed platypus. He could hardly talk. He was in real pain. 'Hold on, colour, I'll ring the med centre.' I got through to the MO and explained the colour sergeant had been attacked by a swarm of wasps and was badly stung. A couple of minutes later, the MO turned up with an orderly in an ambulance. They led the colour sergeant to the ambulance and carted him off to hospital. Fuck me, Loopy could have killed the colour sergeant. Fuck crossing Loopy, I thought.

Everybody heard about the colour sergeant's misfortunes, and more than one squaddie had a good laugh at the colour sergeant's expense. I heard the colour sergeant was going to be alright and would be out of hospital in a couple of days. I also heard the colour sergeant never heard anything before the swarm got him. His thoughts must have been elsewhere. Looks like Loopy got away with this one.

It was a lovely sunny morning when our company started to board the coaches which were parked up on the drill square. Kenny and I sat next to each other for the journey to Changi Airport. All the lads seemed happy to be going home, but I think most of them enjoyed our two and a half years' tour in the Far East.

On the 23rd February 1967, we departed Malaysia. After our battalion's tour of the Far East, we returned to England. Our new barracks were in Tidworth, Hampshire. Time and years were flying by. It was now 1969 and troubles are breaking out all over Northern Ireland. The Protestants and Catholics were at each other's throats and there were sectarian murders on both sides, barricades of stolen burnt-out cars blocking roads leading to their own segregated areas. There was complete unrest in Northern Ireland. My battalion was on 'Spearhead' when the troubles broke out. 'Spearhead' means the battalion is on standby twenty-four hours a day, battle-prepared, ready to go anywhere in the world in times of trouble.

We got sent to Belfast. I was a young soldier and didn't quite understand why we were getting sent there and why we might have to fight our own people. In the early days the Protestants and Catholics didn't know whose side we were on. We tried our best to be fair to both sides; after all, they were our people. Our battalion served four months in Belfast, and we only sustained a few minor injuries. No one was shooting or trying to blow us up yet. The whole battalion learned a lot from those four months that would completely change some of our tactics and our training. When we finished our tour, the battalion returned to Tidworth in Hampshire.

Tidworth is an army garrison on the edge of Salisbury Plain; it's a large military training area with lots of small army training camps dotted all over the place. I was in 1 Platoon, A Company and we were going for a two-week exercise, and we would be locating ourselves in one of these camps. A platoon consists of a platoon commander – which is normally a second lieutenant, a sergeant, three full corporals, three lance corporals and eighteen riflemen or privates. Also you would have a radio operator and a runner. Roughly twenty-eight men, although some platoons might be a little stronger in manpower.

We arrived at our training camp on a freezing cold November's day. We would all be shacked up in a large Nissen hut, which had two pot-bellied stoves, one at each end of the building. This was the only warmth we would have. 'Bliss'. Two weeks of freezing our bollocks off, and to top it all, we would be living off 'compo': tinned food (tinned spuds, tinned meat, tinned cheese), everything in fucking tins. Nothing fresh. With twenty-plus squaddies snoring and farting all night. The platoon commander would have his own bunk – in the officers' mess – and the sergeant would be in the sergeants' mess. Just us squaddies left to slum it.

We were out training daily and we spent a couple of nights out in the woods. Most evenings we were allowed to go to the NAAFI and have a few beers. We only had a few days left before we had to go back to Tidworth. It was a Friday night and a corporal mate of mine was sitting in the NAAFI having a pint. I grabbed a beer and sat next to him. 'Hi, H,' he greeted me. I tell you what he said: 'I'm pissed off with living off compo, I'd do anything for some fresh meat.

'Know how you feel, mate,' I said.

'Look, H, I've brought my air rifle with me, how would you like to come with me and shoot a few pheasants? I've already spoke to the cook and he said if I got one for him he would cook us up a good scran.'

'How? I've never shot a pheasant in my life' I said.

Ray was the corporal's name, and he said, 'We will go out about two am. You carry a large torch and sack and I'll do the shooting.

'Okay, Ray, give me a knock when you're ready.'

Ray woke me up quietly. It was two am. We donned our combats and pumps (not boots). Grabbing his .22 air rifle, and me a torch and sack, off we went a hunting, leaving twenty-plus sleeping squaddies in their Nissen hut snoring and farting the night away.

Crossing fields and climbing hedges, it was a full moon that night so it was quite easy seeing where we were going. Ray seemed to know exactly where to go. He knew where the pheasants would be roosting. 'Over here, H,' he whispered. 'Look,' he said, pointing up at this tree. I could see a pheasant silhouetted against the sky. It was winter, not many leaves left on the trees, so it was easy to spot them. I shone the torch in the eyes of a big old cock pheasant. It looked down the beam of light, frozen, not moving, until my mate (a good shot) rested the .22 rifle on my shoulder, aimed up at the beam of light and shot the bird right in the head. It doesn't always kill them, sometimes just stuns, so when it fell from the tree, squawking, I jumped on it and wring its neck to make sure it's dead. This done, I put it in the sack. Several birds later, a job well done, we started back, looking forward to fresh meat for dinner. We were tiptoeing into the Nissen hut, keeping quiet and freezing our nuts off, when my mate, in his wisdom, decided to look into the sack of pheasants. Whoosh, this big pissed-off cock pheasant, half-strangled and shot in the head came squawking and screaming out of the sack. Blood and feathers flying, it lands on one of the sleeping squaddies' face. With a blood-curdling scream, the woken squaddie, face full of shit, grabs the pheasant off his face and throws it in the air. I switched the lights on as twenty-plus half-drunken and tired squaddies started waking up to see me and Ray trying to catch the pheasant. Mayhem ensues.

The manic pheasant, flying around the Nissen hut for its life, crashed once more into another squaddie, who was on a top bunk. Reaching out he tried to grab it; the squaddie leaned over too far and went crashing to the floor, nutting his mate on the way down. Anything that wasn't tied down was used to throw at the pheasant. Brushes, shovels, sand buckets, not all finding the right target. One squaddie, with a well-aimed hobnailed steel-toed boot slung with all his might, hit the pheasant full on, putting it finally to rest. The boot, however, continued its journey and hit a sleeping squaddie (who had managed to stay asleep in the mayhem) right in his snoring gob. He sat up in bed and removed the boot now lying in his lap and screamed, 'Who the fu—' (two teeth flew out of his gob) '—ck threw the fu— (one more tooth) '—cking boot at my kipper? What the fuck's going on?' No lost teeth that last time. He was not amused at all.

Anyway, the next day we gave the cook his pheasants and he cooked us up a lovely stew. I'd never had pheasant stew before, but it was good after all the compo shit we'd been eating. The guy with the missing teeth ended up in the dentist's chair. After two weeks of freezing our nuts off, the platoon returned to Tidworth. Back in Tidworth, normal infantry training was going on throughout the battalion until the old man (colonel) got the nod that we were going for another tour to Northern Ireland in several months' time. That meant the battalion would, from that moment, be doing intensive Northern Ireland training.

I was a section commander, now a full corporal, in A Company. I was sitting in the guardroom chatting to the lads on guard when my platoon sergeant came into the guardroom. On seeing me he said, 'H, the *RSM (regimental sergeant major) wants to see you straight away, and before you ask, no, I haven't got a clue what for.'

'Fuck me,' I said, 'he's going to give me shit when he sees the length of my hair.'

'That's your fucking fault, I've been telling you all week to get a haircut, but you never listen, now you're are for it,' replied the Sergeant.

It was half eleven when I was knocking on the razz man's door, shitting myself. 'Come in!' he yelled. (Razz Men don't talk, they scream and shout).

On entering his office, I snapped to attention and said, 'Corporal H reporting for duty as ordered, sir.'

He stood up from behind his desk, walked over to me, put his face almost in mine and yelled, 'Am I hurting you, corporal?'

I thought, here we go. The old ones are always the best. 'No, sir' I said.

'Well, I fucking should be,' yelled the razz man. 'I'm standing on your hair. Get a fucking hair cut' he continued.

'Yes, sir,' I said.

'Anyway,' said the razz man, 'the CO wants to see

you.' Bleeding hell, the old man wants to see me. I was startled. It's not very often the CO sends for anyone unless they are in the shite. 'What have you been up to?' growled the razz man.

'Nothing, sir,' I said. 'I haven't got a clue why he wants to see me.'

Still growling, he said, 'Right, be outside the CO's office at 1200 hours, be smartly dressed and get a fucking haircut.' With that said, he barged past me on his way to scream at some other poor bastard.

Get a haircut? It was 1130 then and I had to be outside the CO's office in thirty minutes, I was in the shit even before I see the CO, the razz man was going to nick me because there was no way I could get a haircut and get into my best uniform in such a short time.

The stumpy little fat Geordie get. Everyone called the razz man 'the poison dwarf'. He came screaming at you, spluttering in your face, and, to top that, talking Geordie. I couldn't understand the twat half the time.

1200 hours, standing outside the CO's office, half a pound of Brylcreem on my hair, trying to slick it down, blood running down my neck where I'd tried to cut my hair with my razor. Here we fucking go, I thought as the razz man came out of the CO's office, leaving the door open. I had to do a left turn, then another to get into the CO's office. 'Stand ready' yelled the razz man. 'To the left, quick march, left right, left right,' he yelled. 'Left turn.' Marching into the CO's office, I thought, I've still got my beret on, so I can't be in trouble. If I was in the shit, I would have been told to remove my beret. 'Mark time, left right, left right.' I was marking time just in front of the CO's desk. 'Left right, left right, halt,' yelled the razz man. 'Salute the commanding officer,' he continued.

After I saluted the old man, the razz man said, 'Corporal H for interview, sir,' saluting the CO at the same time.

'Thank you, regimental sergeant major, you may leave now and kindly shut the door behind you.' God, I thought, that's going to upset the razz man, getting politely kicked out of my interview. He's going to give me double shit when I get out of here. I know he noticed I never had a haircut and he would give me the third degree about what the old man had to say to me. The razz man left the room and closed the door behind him.

Just me and the old man. I was intrigued. 'Relax, Corporal H,' said the colonel. 'Pull that chair across and sit down will you.'

Fuckin hell, I thought, what's going on?

'Right Corporal H, I will come straight to the point. You've most likely heard the battalion is going back to Ireland in several months' time?'

'Yes, sir.'

'Well, the powers that be have instructed me to release one of my corporals for the forthcoming tour of Northern Ireland. It's not just my battalion but several battalion commanders have been given the same request. Well, I've chosen you, because I think you will fit the bill and you will carry the flag, so to speak, for the battalion. Listen, H, there is a top secret unit being set up in Northern Ireland. I really don't know much about it at the moment, but what I do know, I'm telling you. Before I go on, this is strictly voluntary. Are you interested?'

Fuck me, of all the corporals in our battalion he chooses me! 'Yes, sir,' I said.

The old man continued, 'This secret unit will initially have about twenty members. When the time arrives, you will be sent on a few courses – surveillance, close quarter combat, small arms and such, so you will be kept busy until you join this new unit. The boss of this unit will be known just as that, the boss, no surnames will be used. You will be working in all areas of Northern Ireland and, H, I've been instructed to tell you, it won't be easy and will at times be extremely dangerous. You will be rubbing shoulders with the IRA in some very volatile areas. Right, H, after all that good news, this is the time to change your mind. Do you accept this tour with this unit?'

'Yes, sir,' I said.

'Okay, H. From now on, until you go to Belfast, you will not wear uniform. You can grow your hair,' he said, smiling at my attempted butchery of cutting my own hair. 'You can grow it past your shoulders, if that's what you want. You can grow a beard, moustache and look as scruffy as you want. You have got eight months of training and to stop behaving like a soldier. I should have more information in a month or so. I will send for you as I receive it.'

I almost broke out laughing, no fucking haircuts, wait till I tell the razz man – he'll go into a fit. 'That's all, H, and good luck with your training.'

I stood up and gave the old man the last salute I would be giving for a while. 'Thank you, sir.' I did an about-turn and marched to the door, opened it and marched right into the waiting razz man. The razz man closed the CO's door then turned round to give me an ear-bashing.

'Who cut your hair?' he shouted. 'Sweeney fuckin' Todd?' The blood was now dry on my collar. Before I could explain, he said, 'Right, to the barber's shop, and when it's cut, report back to me, so I can check it.' Fuck me, here we go again I thought.

'I can't do that, sir,' I said.

'What the fuck you mean you "can't do that"?' Veins were sticking out of his neck, eyes bulging, ready to throw a fit.

'Well, sir, I've been instructed by the colonel not to have a haircut, to grow a beard if I want, and not to wear uniform again until after our forthcoming Ireland tour is over, and to act as though I'm not in the army.'

The 'poison dwarf' looked at me in sheer disbelief. He couldn't believe what he was hearing. It was the first time I've seen the razz man stuck for words. Spluttering and bursting a blood vessel, he screamed at me to get out of his sight. 'Fuck off, you long-haired piece of shite.' He was still yelling at me as I ran out of the HQ block. I'm sure the commanding officer, behind his closed door, was having a right old laugh at the razz man's outbursts.

My first course was a three-week interrogation technique course with the Royal Military Police, based in Bulford, which is only a couple of miles from Tidworth. The 'Monkeys', as the RMPs were called, were hated throughout the entire British army; however, about a week through my course I became friendly with a couple of them and my views changed. I realised they, like the rest of us, had a job to do. They really opened my eyes to how thorough and professional they were, and the RMP sergeant major, who was teaching me, knew his stuff, and by the time my three-week course was up I was comfortable in the knowledge I could do a good job in any interrogation room. At the end of my course, the RMP sergeant major said 'well done' and shook my hand; he said he hoped that what he had taught me would be of use to me. 'You have really opened my eyes,' I said to the sergeant major. I didn't call him sir or sergeant major, just said thanks and then I returned to my battalion in Tidworth, my first course under my belt.

I had just recently met a girl from Liverpool, and we got on really well together, but because of all these courses I had to do, I supposed it would be a while before I got to see her again. Anyway, it was Friday night and my course was finished so I thought I would go across to the corporals' mess for a few pints. I was in the mess, enjoying a pint of lager, when my mate and his wife came in.

'Hello, H,' Ron, my mate, greeted me.

'Hi, folks, come in and sit down and I'll get you both a bevvy. What do you want, Ron?'

'I'll have half a pint of lager and Suzy will have a glass, cheers H.' Suzy was Ron's wife, and she was almost as attractive as my girl back in Liverpool. I got their drinks and we all sat round chatting.

'Fuck me, your hair is growing over your shoulders. I bet you are pissing the razz man off.'

'I try to keep out of his way', I said, smiling.

'How's your new girlfriend?' asked Suzy. 'Nancy's her name, isn't it?'

'Fine,' I said, 'but we are missing each other, and it will be a few months before I can get up to Liverpool to see her.'

My mate and his wife lived in married quarters in Sidbury Circular Road, a large married quarter area about a quarter of a mile from our barracks. His surname was Ramsbottom and everyone called him 'sheep's arse', but not to his face – he was a hard little get.

'Why don't you ask her to come down for a weekend?' Suzy said. 'We've got a spare room, and we could all go out for a meal, I'm sure she would enjoy herself.'

'Good idea,' piped up Ron, 'bring her down, H.'

'Thanks folks, but I don't think Nancy's mum would let her come till she gets to know me better, but I'll phone and ask anyway.'

'Right,' said Ron, lifting his glass, 'let's get drunk.'

'Yeh, why not?' I said.

The next day, waking up with a hangover and after finishing my ablutions, I phoned Nancy and asked her if she could come to stay with me for a couple of days. 'Hang on, I'll just go and ask Mum,' she said. A few seconds later, she came back to the phone and told me her mum said she couldn't come down, but I would be welcome to visit Liverpool anytime I wanted.

'It will be a few months before I can come up to Liverpool, Nancy,' I said.

'When Mum gets to know you better, everything will be fine. She knows how I feel about you, she knows I love you.'

'I love you too, Nancy,' I said.

We chatted for a while longer and then we both said our goodbyes.

'Bye for now, H. Write me a nice long letter. Love you.'

'I will write, I promise. I love you, Nancy,' I said, and rang off. I loved this Scouse girl.

The weeks were flying by now, and I still had three more courses to do. My next course was with our battalion's photographic section. I had to learn how to use a camera with zoom lenses. It was a two-week course and it was very interesting as I'd never used a camera before. Stu, the battalion photographer, took me all over the training area, showing me how to use the cameras. We took snaps of tanks, soldiers training and some of the local wildlife. The photographs I took Stu developed and showed me my work, saying, 'These snaps are not bad at all. You can keep them, H.'

'Thanks, Stu,' I said.

'The CO wants photographs of you.'

'What for?' I said.

'I don't know, but what the CO wants he gets, so put a smile on your kipper, H,' Stu said, lifting the camera into position. After taking my mugshot, Stu offered me his hand, saying, 'Well done, H, that's the course finished.'

I shook Stu's hand and said, 'Thanks, mate, I really enjoyed it. You've taught me a load of good stuff.'

A week later, I was sent to the garrison gym for a week's close quarter combat course. This course was normally two weeks long, but because I had already done this course while I was in Malaya, it was more of a top-up than instruction. The instructor taught me some terrible ways of maiming and killing. As a soldier it's your duty to survive any way you can; that's why you get taught this scary stuff. It's not a sport.

It would only be three months before our battalion would be deployed to Northern Ireland. I watched the lads training and on more than one occasion I was shoved up against the wall and searched, because I had long hair and was in civvies. I sometimes played enemy and had a pistol or rounds on me. It helped the squaddies in their training. My mate was training round the camp with his section when he got two of his lads to put me up against a wall yet again and search me. They really gave me the once-over. Taff was the corporal in charge. 'Fuck me, Taff,' I said, 'not so rough.'

'Just training, H,' he said, 'just training,' while grinning at his lads.

It was Thursday afternoon when the old man sent for

me. My platoon sergeant told me to be outside the old man's office by 1500 hours. At 1450 hours I entered the HQ block, heading towards the CO's office when I noticed the razz man's door was ajar. I swiftly walked past his office as I didn't want him to see me; I didn't want to antagonise him with the way I looked. I knocked on the CO's door. 'Enter' said the voice on the other side of the door. I opened the door, walked into the office, closing the door behind me. 'Hello,' greeted the colonel. 'Grab that chair,' he said, 'and sit down.'

'Thank you, colonel,' I said.

'The battalion will be deployed in three months' time, as you know. You, however, will be going to Northern Ireland three weeks before the rest of us. When the time comes you will get the train to Liverpool and then the ferry to Belfast. When you arrive in Belfast there will be a couple of lads from your new unit waiting for you at the terminal. The battalion photographer supplied me with a couple of photographs of you, which I in turn will send to the boss of your unit. The lads picking you up will know you, but just in case, you will be issued with a password to take with you. You will then be driven to your unit to meet your boss and its other members. Your unit will supply you with arms and ammunition, and when you've had a full briefing, you will be ready to do what you've been trained to do. As I told you in my last brief, you will address the CO as "boss" – there will be no rank and no surnames. You okay with that, H?'

'Yes, colonel,' I said.

'You've only got one more course to do – surveillance and countersurveillance – which you will be doing with the Royal Military Police at Bulford. I hear you made a couple of friends on the interrogation course?' the CO said with a glint in his eye.

'Yes, colonel, the Monkey RMPs aren't too bad once you get to know them.'

'Okay, H, I'll most likely see you again before you go. That's all for now.'

I stood up and said, 'Thank you, colonel' and left his office, closing the door behind me.

I was trying to sneak past the razz man's open door when he spotted me. 'Get in here, you long-haired get' shouted the razz man. I walked into the RSM's office. He got up from behind his desk and walked over to me. 'I've known all along what you have been training for and what you will be doing in Northern Ireland,' he said. The razz man extended his hand out in front of him. I shook his hand. I was shocked. The razz man smiled at me and said, 'Good luck, H, keep your head down. You can go now.' Turning and walking out of his office, I thought fuck me, it's got a heart, and it smiles.

There were eight of us on the surveillance course, and I was the only one who wasn't an RMP. Our instructor was the same sergeant major who taught me my interrogation techniques. After a very interesting five days in the classroom, the sergeant major said, 'Right, lads, the weekend is here, so enjoy it. See you 0800 Monday for the second half of the course.'

After the weekend, we practised a lot of what we had been taught: how to follow a person without being seen, how to spot someone who might be following you. The instructor showed us all the techniques and what everyday things we could use to our advantage. I learned a lot more stuff on this course. It was very interesting, and I enjoyed it. The more I worked with the

RMPs, the more I got to like them. The knowledge the instructors passed on to me would certainly come in handy in Northern Ireland. After the course I said my goodbyes to the lads, thanked the sergeant major once again and returned to my battalion in Tidworth. Well, that was it. All my courses over, just have to wait now for my deployment date and I'd be off.

*

We were in October now and I knew it would only be a matter of days before my deployment. It was Monday morning; I was in the company office chatting to the clerk and my platoon sergeant when the phone rang. The clerk answered the phone and after a couple of seconds said, 'Yes, sir, he's here now, I will put you on to him.' The clerk handed me the phone saying, 'The chief clerk wants to talk to you.'

'Thanks, mate,' I said, taking the phone off him. 'H here,' I said into the mouthpiece.

The chief clerk said, 'Come over to my office, I've got your deployment orders.'

'Thanks, chief, I will be across in five minutes,' I said, putting the phone down. 'I've got my deployment orders,' I said to my platoon sergeant.'

'Good luck, mate,' he said.

I made my way over to the HQ block where the chief clerk's office is situated. His office was the last one at the end of a long corridor, past the razz man's and CO's offices. I reached the chief clerk's, knocking on his door and entering his office. I walked over to where the chief clerk was sitting.

'Hi, H,' he greeted. 'Sit down, and I will go over your orders.' I grabbed a chair and sat down opposite the chief. The chief started, 'You will be leaving this Wednesday at

1300 hours, and the MT section will drive you to Andover station, where you will get the train to Liverpool. Then you will get the evening ferry to Belfast. On arriving in Belfast, you will be met by two guys of your new unit. Their names are Bill and Charlie. They have got your photograph so they should be able to spot you. Just to make sure it's the right guys, you will have a password as a backup. The password is sunny————-July. All this is written down for you, so you can get it fixed in your mind. In your orders, you've got train timings, ferry timings, everything I've just told you. You okay with this, H?.'

'Yes I am, thanks chief.'

The chief pushed an envelope across his desk towards me, saying, 'When you've got it all in your head, destroy it. There's also an advance of pay to keep you going.'

'Thanks again, chief.'

*

It was a cold Wednesday morning. I was standing outside A Company office when my car turned up from the MT section to take me to the railway station. The car pulled up beside me and the driver got out saying, 'Throw your kit in the boot, H.' It was the colonel's driver and the colonel's car.

I said to Dave, the CO's driver, 'Bloody hell, mate, you are sending me off in style here,' while climbing into the car. Dave said that he'd been told by the CO to pick me up and to wish me good luck. 'Thanks, mate,' I said.

Arriving at Andover station, Dave pulled the car over and we got out. He opened the boot, took out my small case and handed it to me, saying, 'I hope you have a safe tour, mate.'

'Thanks Dave.' Shaking his hand, I said, 'Thanks for the lift.'

'No problem, mate,' he said as he got back into the car, giving me a wave as he drove away.

I went over to a payphone outside the station. I thought I'd give Nancy a ring. After a few rings, the phone was answered by her mum.

'Hello, Ma,' I said. 'Could I speak to Nancy?' I called her Ma and she didn't seem to mind.

'Hello, H,' she greeted, 'I'll get her for you.' I could hear Ma shouting for Nancy and I could hear Nancy running down the stairs.

Nancy said, 'Hello, I'm missing you so much.'

'I'm missing you too,' I told her. I said, 'I'm just about to get on the train to Liverpool. I've got to make a couple of exchanges on the way, but as soon as I get to Liverpool, I'll ring you again. I'm on the evening ferry and it sails at 2230, but I've got to be on board an hour before sailing.'

'Can I see you when you get here?' she said.

I told her my schedule was tight, but I should have at least an hour to see her. 'I will meet you in the café at the terminal. Because it will be late, can Steven come with you to keep you company?' I said, 'and look after you for me?'

'Mum would make him come with me anyway,' Nancy said. We told each other of our love and then I rang off, saying, 'Say hello to your family for me, I love you.'

Sitting on the train as it pulled out of the station, mind in overdrive, I was looking forward to seeing Nancy. I was thinking about my new unit, what it was going to be like, all kinds of stuff going through my mind, when I must have closed my eyes and slept. I slept for a good hour because when I checked my watch it was ten past three. I left Andover at two o'clock.

I knew when I got to Crewe, I had to change trains and that I would have an hour's wait for my next train. I would know then what time I would be arriving in Liverpool, if the trains were on time, I could then phone Nancy and arrange what time to meet her.

It was a long old journey, but having finally reached Crewe, I got off the train and looked for a phone box. When I did find the phone there was a queue of people waiting to use it. No matter, I thought, I'm stuck here for an hour anyway. Eventually getting on the phone, I rang Nancy.

'Hello,' she greeted me.

'Hi, love, I've missed you, I've really missed you.'

'I love you,' she said. 'Where are you?'

'I'm in Crewe. There's no delays to the trains, so everything's going well. I will meet you in the café at 2000 hours— sorry, eight o'clock. We will only have an hour, but don't worry, love, it won't always be like this.'

'An hour is better than nothing,' she said.

'Okay, love, I'll see you eight o'clock. Bye for now, love you, bye.'

On arriving at Liverpool, I jumped a taxi to the ferry terminal. It was twenty to eight when I got there. Looking through the café window, I could see Nancy and Steven sitting down with steaming cups of tea or coffee in their hands. It was a cold evening. On entering the café, I saw Nancy turn and look at me briefly. She then turned back around and carried on talking to Steven. I was in scruff order, long hair past my shoulders, I had a large moustache and stubble on my chin. I was wearing a donkey jacket, collar pulled up with a scarf round the bottom half of my face. I knew she hadn't recognised me. The last time she saw me I had short back and sides. I was looking at her when she turned and looked at me again. I saw recognition appear in her eyes. She almost knocked the table over when she sprang to her feet. We fell into each other's arms, both of us clinging to each other. I gently prised her away from me – I wanted to look into those lovely green eyes, this beautiful creature I had found. I don't know what she saw in me, but I was thankful for it. We kissed and then made our way to where Steven was sitting. 'Hello, Steve,' I said. 'Nice to see you again, and thank you for bringing Nancy.'

We shook hands. 'Hello, H, I never recognised you,' he said.

'Yeh, this is me for the next five months or so,' I said.

Nancy went and got me a cup of tea and we sat round chatting. Steven, finishing his tea, ever the diplomat, said, 'I'm going for a little walk' and that he would be back in half an hour. As he left I reached my hands across the table and took Nancy's hands in mine. We just stared into each other's eyes. Just looking at her, I had a warm feeling going through me. It was a feeling I had never experienced before. I knew I loved this scouse girl. We were talking away when Steven came back.

That thirty minutes flew by. 'I've got to board,' I told Nancy.

'I know,' she said. We both got up, I grabbed my case and the three of us left the café.

Standing by the side of the ferry, I shook Steven's hand and turning to Nancy I took her in my arms and kissed her, both of us with tears in our eyes. Parting, I turned round to Steven and said, 'Take her home, mate, I don't want you two hanging around in the cold for two hours.'

'Okay, H,' he said.

I gave Nancy another hug and kiss, then I turned round and boarded the ferry.

The Unit

It was a rough crossing and I was glad when the ferry finally docked in Belfast. I had skipped breakfast, knowing I would just bring it up again. After about thirty or so minutes of the ship docking, people started to disembark, so I joined the flow.

I left the terminal and was just standing by a row of taxis trying to spot the two lads that were picking me up. I was told in my orders where to wait. I got a tap on my shoulder and, on turning round, I was looking at a broad-shouldered, friendly-faced lad. He said, 'Are you H?'

'Yes,' I said. Then I said, 'Sunny', to which he replied, 'July', the second part of the password.

He said, 'I'm Charlie, and Bill is waiting for us in the car park.' Charlie offered me his hand, which I shook. He said, 'Welcome to the unit, H.'

'Thanks, Charlie.'

Charlie led the way over to the car park and, on reaching it, introduced me to Bill, saying, 'This is the best damn driver I've ever met.'

Bill shook my hand and he also welcomed me to the unit. He opened the rear car door, saying, 'Jump in, H, put your case on the back seat. It will be okay there.' I climbed into the back seat of the car thinking, I like the look of these guys – they look like the kind of guys you want with you in a tight situation. Bill, driving to base, said, 'The journey is about half an hour if the traffic's good.' The lads started to tell me about the unit and the kind of stuff we'd do.

'The boss will give you a full brief when we arrive,' said Charlie.

'Thanks, lads,' I said.

After about thirty minutes we pulled up outside a heavily armed military unit. We had to get out of the car while it – and us – got searched. When the squaddies finished, they said, 'Okay, lads, in you go.'

Getting back in the car, Bill pulled away and drove us to the far side of the military unit, saying, 'We are based far from any of the other soldiers.' He pulled the car over outside two large gates, which were getting opened for us to drive through. Bill drove through the gates and said, 'Thanks, spanner,' to the guy who had just opened the gates. He pulled the car over and parked the car next to several more cars which were parked on the right-hand side of the camp. We all got out of the car and Charlie and Bill went over to the left-hand side of the gate, where a load of sandbags formed a V shape.

Bill and Charlie both had 9mm pistols, which they took out of their shoulder holsters. They pointed their pistols at the sandbags and unloaded them. Charlie looked at the puzzled look on my face and said, 'The guards on the gate know us. It's just a pretend search for any prying eyes. Come on, I'll show you your bunk, you can dump your kit and I'll take you to meet the boss.' After dumping my kit, Charlie led me over to a large hut, saying, 'This is our HQ.' There were a half-dozen lads coming and going round the camp all saying 'hello' or nodding their heads on passing. We entered the HQ block and were greeted by a large guy, at least six foot two in height. Charlie said, 'Hi, boss, this is H, our newest member.'

'Thanks, Charlie, you can go now.' The boss came over to shake my hand. 'Welcome, H, grab a seat and we'll have a little chat.' The boss began, 'We are a newish unit, but already we have become a thorn in the IRA's side. Our main job is spying on suspects and getting as much information as we can about them. All info we get we pass on to several intelligence officers working in Northern Ireland. One such intelligence officer works here with the resident battalion, and we meet almost every day. We have got lots of *"ops" all over Belfast, and some of our lads are out there now. We had an incident last week when one of our lads dispatched an IRA man. There's newspapers in the rest room – when you get five minutes, have a read about it, it made the headlines. For your first week here you will be going out with the lads every day. They will show you the ropes and you will get to know the guys. You most likely saw, when you entered camp, that we have several cars. These are kept in good working order by the spanner, our mechanic. Three of these cars are fitted out with a secret compartment large enough to hold a mugshot folder and such, and they are also fitted with a two-way radio. If you go out in a car on ops, there will normally be three of you. Obviously the driver, the commander – who sits in the front passenger seat – and the machine gunner in the back. Later today, you will be issued with a 9mm Browning pistol and thirty rounds of ammunition off Rob, who is our clerk and armourer. After your week out with the lads, I will ease you into your first job. I will put you in an op with Jacko. He's been out half a dozen times so far, so he knows the ropes. Jacko is in camp at the moment so look him up and introduce yourself to him and anyone else you come across. Your mugshots are up with all the rest of the lads on the wall in the briefing room, so everyone should know who you are. Any questions, H?'

'No, boss,' I said.

'Right then, H, before you go, here is an address. If any of your family write, this is the address they must write to, and your mail will be passed on to us.' I took the card off the boss, thanked him and headed for my bunk to unpack.

In my bunk unpacking, there was a knock on my door. I was just about to say come in when the door opened and in walked, I assumed, one of the lads. He had a big grin on his face. 'Hi, H, I'm Jacko,' he said. We shook hands and he plonked himself on the end of my bed. 'Right, mate,' he said, 'after a week out with the lads showing you the area and such, you and I will be going into one of our ops. The boss will brief us when the time comes. I've done this op a couple of times now with one of the lads. There's a doctor that came up from the south and set up a practice in a right dodgy area. Anyway, he's on our radar, so we are keeping an eye on him.'

'Sounds interesting,' I said.

Then a complete change of subject. Jacko pulled a photograph out of his wallet. He handed it to me and said, 'What do you think of them then, mate?'

I looked at the photograph and it was a photo, I assumed, of his wife and three daughters. His wife was an attractive lady and his three girls were beautiful.

'That's a lovely looking family,' I said. 'How old are the kids?'

'Six, seven and eight,' he said. Keeps the wife busy.

Anyway, H, I thought I would beat you to the introduction. I'll leave you to unpack.'

'Cheers, Jacko,' I said.

Later, Bill came into my room, saying, 'Come on, H, I'll show you round the compound.' We walked outside and Bill said, 'I see you have already met Jacko.'

'Yes,' I said. 'I bet he showed you a photograph of his wife and kids?'

'He did, how did you know that?' I said.

'He shows everyone,' Bill said, smiling. 'He's besotted with them.' After Bill showed me round the compound, he said, 'See you in the NAAFI hut later.'

'Okay, Bill, and thanks,' I said.

Our compound was tucked away on a large military base near Newtownards where very few people could see our comings and goings – only the guards on the gate, and they were well briefed. It was a large compound with twelve feet of corrugated iron sheets all the way round. It had rolls of barbed wire across the top. The compound was entered through two large gates. Through the gates on the right hand side of the compound was a car park housing several cars and a small workshop where the spanner could fix the cars when they needed it. Further down towards the rear of the compound were three large huts, each with eight small bunks. The bunks were basic: a locker, bed, a bedside locker and a small hand basin. Next, another small hut, which the lads called the NAAFI hut. This served as our eating and relaxing area. It had several easy chairs scattered round. There were three tables, each with four chairs. It housed a TV, and there were a couple of bookshelves with an assortment of books, papers and magazines. There was also a large fridge. On the left hand side of the gate, in the corner, was the loading and unloading bay. This consisted of sandbags stacked three deep, about eight feet across and five feet high. Just past this was our HQ and briefing hut. Further down on the left was a large metal container with a sturdy looking door on each end of it. Each side of the door had two large metal hoops. Through these hoops was a large metal rod that was bent into an L shape on one end, so it could not pass through the metal hoop. The other end had a large padlock attached to it. It was the same on both doors. The container was divided into two compartments by a partition. This served as our armoury, one side for ammunition and the other for weapons. The last hut on the left was the ablutions hut.

This was to be our home for the duration of our tour. I was walking back towards my bunk when Rob called me over to him, saying, 'Come on, H, I will issue you with your weapon. I will give you a 9mm Browning to start with. You can change weapons to suit your task anytime. As you know, if you are dressed in shit order, donkey jacket and stuff, you can hide the larger 9mm easier. If you are wearing a suit, the Walther PPK is more suitable.'

'Yeh, thanks, Rob,' I said as I followed him to the armoury. Reaching the armoury, Rob unlocked the large lock and slid the bolt across and out of the metal loops. He opened the doors and we entered the container. I looked around the container and was shocked at the amount of fire power we had at our disposal.

Rob sensing, what I was thinking, said, 'Not bad, hey, H?'

'Not bad at all,' I said.

Rob passed me over a 9mm, saying, 'Sign for it on that book on the desk over there. You can also sign for thirty rounds of ammunition and three magazines. I've already done the paperwork, just needs signing. I'll give you your ammunition and magazines in a minute.'

'Okay, Rob,' I said as I signed the book. Rob then led the way to the other end of the container, closing and locking the armoury doors behind him.

I checked the 9mm Browning Rob issued me with. It was well-oiled and sparkling clean. Rob opened up the other end of the container and led the way into the ammo compound where he gave me my three magazines and thirty rounds of ammunition.

'Thanks Rob, I feel dressed now.'

'You might as well take a shoulder holster as well, H. Most pistols will fit into these holsters, although the only pistols we have are the 9mm and Walther. The holsters are not everyone's cup of tea, but some of the lads do wear them. If you feel you don't like wearing it, just leave it in your room.'

'Okay, Rob, and thanks again,' I said as I shook his hand.

My first trip into Belfast was to familiarise me with the area we would be working in. Bill was doing the driving and Charlie was the commander. I was in the back of the car. I liked working with these two lads. Bill drove to the Royal Victoria Hospital and they pointed out where the military wing was. Some of the areas we drove round made the hair on the back of my neck stick up. We drove past the doctor's practice, the one we were keeping an eye on. About five hundred metres past the doctor's, Charlie pointed out a disused factory and said, 'We have a good vantage point in there. Its where we are watching the good doctor. The op is not continually used, just when the boss says so. The army lads know when we are in the op and have some lads on standby to pull us out if we ever get bumped.'

'That's nice to know,' I said.

'Yeh. Okay, I know a nice little café in a safe area,' said Bill.

'Sounds good to me, I could do with a nice bacon banjo,' I said.

The next few days, I got to know Belfast better. The Protestant areas and Catholic areas. What a shame in this day and age that people kill and maim in the name of religion. I think the world would be better off without it. It was getting towards the weekend, I was sitting in my room writing a letter when Jacko came in, saying, 'Come on, H, the boss wants a chat.' Putting my pen and half written letter on my bedside locker, I stood up and followed Jacko to see the boss.

'What's going on?' I asked.

Jacko said, 'It's going to be your first job, and the boss is going to give us a quick brief.'

Walking into the briefing room, the boss was already sitting behind his desk at the front of the room. 'Sit down, lads,' the boss said, smiling. The boss seemed to have a permanent smile on his face; he was a likeable boss, but you could feel the power of the man when you were in his presence. I bet many a man has regretted misjudging this guy. 'Right, H,' said the boss, 'I'm going to send you out on your first job with Jacko here. Jacko has already done this job a few times, so he knows the ropes. You two are going to do an op on the doctor's surgery. We have already got good intel on him, but we want more photographs of the comings and goings of people visiting his practice, especially at night. You will be going in tomorrow night. On this occasion there will only be the two of you, and you will be doing your own driving. There's a street close to the op where there's always loads of cars parked. That's where you will park up and then walk to the op. You will get yourselves into the op by 1800 hours and stay until around midnight or just after, according to what's going on. The local army lads have been briefed what time you will be occupying the op, and I will let them know when you leave. If you get bumped in the op, the squaddies will come in and get you out. They will be on standby for the duration of your stay in the op. Like I said, Jacko knows the ropes, he's got a rucksack to carry your camera and bits and pieces and don't forget your plastic bags. Any questions?'

'No, boss,' we both said.

'If you squeeze a shit out before you go, or use a bung tablet – loperamide, they are called – you won't need the plastic bags, but take them with you anyway,' the boss said. Okay, lads, that's it for now, good luck.'

'Thanks, boss,' we both said in unison.

1630 hours, the next day, the spanner came into the rest room where Jacko and I and a few of the other lads were relaxing. He came over to us and handed Jacko a set of car keys saying, 'Your car for tonight is the dark red Vauxhall. I've checked her out, it's running good and all fuelled up.'

'Thanks, spanner,' replied Jacko.

'Bring her back in one piece,' said the spanner, smiling as he left the room.

Jacko and I had already prepared our kit for the op. Camera, tripod, spare roll of film, torch with a red disc on the torch's face, binoculars, sandwiches and water, two-way radio, and we were both carrying 9mm Browning pistols, both well cleaned and oiled, both cocked with a round up the spout, safety catch on. We were ready should we get bumped.

At 1700 hours Jacko and I drove out the gates of our compound, Jacko behind the wheel. The spanner gave us a wave as he closed the gates behind us. After about forty minutes of dodging in and out of the traffic, we reached our destination. We were lucky to find a convenient parking space a short walk from our op. After looking up and down the street for a few minutes, we got out of the car, locked it and after another quick look around, we headed for our op. Jacko led the way; he knew the route in where we were less likely to be spotted. He picked his way through the ruins of the disused factory and the scurrying rats. We had to be very wary, because it was places like this where the IRA hid their weapons, and also if we got spotted going in, the IRA would have a nice little booby trap or some sort of surprise the next time we used it. We were both dressed in donkey jackets and overalls and hopefully, if we did get spotted by some passerbys, they would think we were a couple of workers taking a shortcut across the old factory grounds. We came up to a flight of concrete stairs and I followed Jacko up them. We crossed a massive room with all kinds of debris all over the place. Jacko picked his way through the debris, knowing exactly where to tread, causing the minimum amount of noise. I followed in Jacko's tracks up to another flight of steps. After climbing these and three more flights of stairs, we reached our destination. We came up to a smallish room with its door hanging ajar from one remaining rusty hinge. The other hinge had long ago rusted away. Jacko whispered for me to wait by the open door while he checked the room out. He knew where every brick, every piece of wood and debris was. He checked everything carefully and eventually waved me in. I was just about to enter the room when two rats scurried right over my feet. It took a bit of willpower to stop me screaming at the rats and kicking out at them. Gingerly, I entered the room. 'This is it, H, come and have a dekko out of the window,' he said, as he handed me the binoculars.

I stood back away from the window in the shadow of the room and raised the binoculars to my eyes as Jacko steered me to where the doctor's surgery was. 'Fuck me, these are powerful binoculars, I can see everything very clearly,' I said to Jacko.

Jacko got two small crates and put a plank of wood across them, saying, 'This is our makeshift seat for the next few hours.' Jacko then left the room, saying he would be back in a few minutes. I continued scanning the surgery. We were bloody high up here; whoever chose this op got it right. After a few minutes, Jacko returned. He must have seen the puzzled look on my face. 'Just put some cans on the stairs and a bit of corrugated iron. It's just a little early warning in case the bastards try to sneak up on us.'

We prepared our kit for the next few hours. Jacko set the camera up on the tripod and zoomed it in on the doctors practice. It was dark outside now, it made me feel a little safer because anyone sneaking around the factory now, besides the rats, was bound to make a noise. 'Right, H, we will take half-hour shifts with the binoculars, it strains your eyes after a while.'

'OK mate,' I said.

Over the next few hours, we would take some very interesting snaps. I know the intel guys would be interested in them.

Belfast, October 1972

The warm liquid burst forth, spreading around my groin. Is this the way it's going to end? The liquid ran down my legs dripping to the floor. My bladder burst, I had pissed myself with fright, I thought I would have been a braver man than this.

Two large men half-dragging, half-carrying me down this dimly lit side street. What was I doing here? What got me into this situation? My head kept getting flash backs. A third man walking in front of us kept pointing a pistol towards me; somehow, I knew it to be a Browning 9mm. This man, it seemed, was leading me to my destiny. As my head started to clear, a woman came from out of nowhere and took the place of one of the men now walking me as my legs were a little steadier. I looked her in the eye and asked, 'Are you going to kill me'? She looked startled. I said, 'I didn't know Protestants killed British soldiers.'

Memories started flooding back: Newtownards Road, Yes that's where we were before I was dragged and carried down this side street. A DOMINANT PROTESTANT AREA. The woman looked a little shocked and said, 'Are you a British soldier?'

'Yes' was all I said.

I was taken down a small alley between a row of terraced houses. At the back of a house, someone opened a door that led into a brightly lit kitchen. I was pushed through the door and roughly pushed down onto a chair next to a large wooden table, two big burly men standing each side of me each with a hand on my shoulder. I was going nowhere. The woman sat opposite me; next to her, pointing a pistol at me, was an evil-looking man, finger on the trigger, his eyes burning right into mine.

Cruel, unfeeling eyes. I don't think he cared if he pulled the trigger or not. There was no compassion, no pity. This man, I'm sure, had killed before. In an adjoining room I could hear lots of raised voices, shouting, arguing. I think these arguments were about my fate. The inner door of the kitchen opened and a head poked through and glared at me then disappeared back behind the door. The woman opposite me, who had never taken her eyes off me, asked again, 'Are you a soldier'? This woman seemed to carry a lot of weight around here.

Again I said, 'Yes.' I knew the gun being pointed at me was my own 9mm Browning, my own weapon. How ironic – it looked like I was going to get a *double tap with my own gun, my own rounds.[2] Although one *round would have been enough.

My piss was starting to smell.

We had just finished a surveillance job on this doctor, who had just moved into Belfast from Dundalk in the south. He seemed a normal family man with two young kids. He had a good reputation as a fine doctor. However, the doctor had a dark secret: we knew he was in the IRA and had patched up more than one wounded IRA man. We took all the relevant snaps of his house, his practice, and car, also the comings and goings of after-surgery-hour visitors. Now it would be a waiting game. I thought he would have felt safer in the south, but for whatever reason, he moved north. Why? That was for us to find out.

Anyway, surveillance over for now, we were returning back to base via the Newtownards Road. Jacko was driving our car, a modified Vauxhall Viva, dark red in colour, and it was fitted out with a hidden two-way radio and a secret compartment big enough to hold a medium-sized folder, about a foot long and eight inches wide.

About fifty-plus *UDA (Ulster Defence Association) vigilantes were patrolling their area. This was quite a common sight in the early days. Most wore hoods, with scarves around their faces. Almost all wore combat jackets, and most carried a weapon of sorts, pick helves or sticks, no guns to be seen – that's not to say they didn't have any. The vigilantes were walking down the left-hand side of the road, the same direction we were travelling in. About three hundred yards in front of us they were crossing the road. They appeared to be leaving a gap for us to drive through. Jacko, my driver, headed towards the gap, then what must have been only a few minutes changed our lives forever.

Travelling about thirty mph, the car suddenly gained speed heading straight towards the gap. I don't know whether Jacko had spotted anything to make him speed up, but I heard what sounded like a pistol shot and at the same time I saw something spinning towards our car windscreen, the lights of the street lamps flashing on the spinning object. I screamed at Jacko to duck as I started to lower myself as much as I could below the console. A terrifying loud crack and the windscreen shattered, showering us with glass. I looked up and saw we had mounted the pavement. The car was out of control, heading towards a telephone box. I yelled at Jacko to control the car. Just before the impact, I turned to look at Jacko, and in that split second, I saw an image, an image I would take to my grave. Poor Jacko.

The smell of my urine still strong (what a thing to think about in my situation), the inner door of the kitchen burst open and in walked four or five men. The first bloke to enter seemed to be in charge. He came over to me and said, 'Are you a soldier?'

'Yes,' I said. 'Can you please take me back to the scene of the accident?'

My mind was fully alert now. I seemed to have recovered all my senses and, as far as I could feel, I had no broken bones. By saying 'accident' they might think I had lost my mind a little and that I thought it was an accident instead of an ambush. After more deliberation between the men, the big bloke said, 'Come on' and before I could stand up, he grabbed me under the arm, almost lifting me off my feet, such was his strength. 'We are taking you back to the crash.'

I'd looked back through the shattered windscreen just before we smashed into the telephone box. The solid side of the telephone box bent over, and we hit a wall. Hitting the phone box before the wall must have saved my life. Like a double impact, the box softened the impact into the wall. Then, for a while, darkness had enveloped me and, when I came to, head spinning, a pistol was being pointed at my head.

The young lad's finger was pulling the trigger. Someone was looking after me: the Browning 9mm had the safety catch on with a round up the spout, and the kid obviously didn't know about the safety catch. A bloke appeared. He punched the kid and grabbed the pistol off him. Still groggy, I was pulled out the car by a couple of men who half-carried, half-dragged me down a dimly lit side street.

The big bloke and some of his mates, along with the woman, surrounded me and started to lead me back up the street towards the scene of the 'accident'. I could see the bright lights of the Newtownards Road a couple of hundred yards in front of me. I knew there would be soldiers at the scene of the ambush. Yes, I can say it, because that's the way it was.

Coming out of the side street, there was the wreck of our car. My entourage held back and let me go forward by myself. Two Land Rovers with two bricks of soldiers were at the scene. My head was full of emotions, glad to be out that side street, glad to see the soldiers, glad to be alive. The soldiers would normally be in all-round defence with rifles at the ready, but because this was a Protestant area, they seemed a little more relaxed, but still fully alert. A brick is a unit containing four soldiers. Normally, two bricks work together – each brick will cover each other, especially across open country. 'A Brick' is made up of a corporal and three men, the second brick, a lance corporal and three men. The full corporal is overall in charge.

However, a major seemed to be in charge of these two bricks. Most of the soldiers were armed with SLR 7.62 rifles, although I noticed the major wore a holstered 9mm Browning pistol.

I went over to the car. Looking into the car, I could see bits of Jacko all over the console, blood everywhere. I held back the nausea and reached for the secret compartment. To my surprise, the compartment wasn't buckled, and opened easily. I grabbed the folder and roll of film and thrust them into the major's arms saying, 'Keep these safe.' After a quick look he put the folder inside his combat jacket and the roll of film in his pocket. He said that my companion was alive but seriously injured and had been taken to the Royal Victoria Hospital. He radioed a military ambulance to take me to hospital. The ambulance arrived, it was a converted Saracen (armoured personnel carrier). I was helped into the ambulance and then I was taken to the same hospital as Jacko – the RVH, as it was called.

The folder I handed to the major was top secret and, in the wrong hands would bring countless repercussions, for it contained top secret intelligence, information on the top five IRA terrorists in our area. It also contained information on the top five *UDA players in our area.

We had photographs of their wives, mistresses, their car registration numbers, addresses, where they drank, telephone numbers, what turned them on and what they were into – arms smuggling, drugs, prostitution, racketeering, just to name a few. It was a seedy, dangerous world they lived in, and religion was just a front. They were all wealthy, evil men living off terrorism. All had blood on their hands. They strutted round their self-made no-go areas, ruling the roost, but not for long if we had anything to do with it. None of them had any idea how much we knew about them, but there was still more information for us to find out, and we would get it. That's why we were there.

Lying in my hospital bed, my mind in turmoil with all kinds of things going through my head. I was in my own little world when the doctor came to my bedside. He said my X-rays were back and everything was okay. Bad bruising to my chest and legs, but no broken bones. He said that because I was knocked out, I would have to stay in hospital for three days for observation. The doctor told me I had a visitor from my unit earlier, but I was sedated so he said he would come back the next day. That said, he moved onto his next patient.

I didn't sleep very well that night. My thoughts kept going back to Jacko, wondering how he was and would he be alright. Eventually, I fell asleep only to be woken up, which felt like only minutes later, but must have been a good few hours.

'Wake up! Wake up!' a booming voice shouted down the corridor – the friendly orderly going about his morning ritual with the full gusto of an *RSM on heat.

'Walking wounded,' he continued shouting, 'get yourselves a shit, shave, shower and then get your own breakfast. I'm not your mother.' Nurses were already passing cups of tea round, tending the bedbound wounded. We were all in the military wing of the Royal Victoria Hospital, two armed soldiers at the entrance to the ward and a strong army presence all over the hospital. The doctors, nurses and orderlies were all military from the Royal Army Medical Corps. I felt safe there. After my ablutions and breakfast, I was relaxing, lying on my bed, when my visitor from the day before came walking towards my bed. It was my boss from our unit. A slim yet powerful-looking man, about six feet two, who had an easy-going way about him. We all had an idea what regiment he came from, but hardly commented about it. It was all first names, and that was okay with everyone. What we didn't know we couldn't divulge should we ever be captured, but then again I would use my last round on myself rather than be taken by a vicious IRA torture gang.

'Hi, H,' he greeted. Resting the bag he was carrying next to my bed, he then sat down on the end of my bed next to me.

'Hi, boss, how's Jacko? Any news?'

'Sorry, H,' he said, 'Jacko is in a coma and in a very bad way and, to be honest with you, there's not much chance he will make it through.' The boss looked at me and said, 'Is there a room with a little privacy where we can talk?' There was a room that was used for visiting families to stay. It was empty at the moment so that's where I took the boss. Entering the room we sat opposite each other at a small table. 'Tell me everything you can remember about the incident, H.'

After a moment to reflect, I began my story. I told him about the gap the UDA had left for us to drive through, and how I didn't understand why Jacko sped up all of a sudden, unless he saw something I'd missed. I tried my best to describe what some of my captors looked like. I gave a good description of the guy in the kitchen pointing my own 9mm pistol at me. One evil-looking get he was, and I was sure he would be in our mugshot gallery back at base. I described the woman and how she seemed to carry a lot of clout; people seemed to obey her every word. I got the number of the house I was held in and also the name of the street. I told the boss that they stole my 9mm pistol and that I gave the intelligence folder and the roll of film to the major at the scene of the ambush. The boss already knew about my 9mm and the intelligence folder and film. No surprise there! The boss didn't have a pencil or notebook with him. He would remember everything I told him, for he was one of those people blessed with a photographic memory. We'd spoken for another fifteen mins or so when the boss stood up and said, 'Let's go back to the ward.' Back at my bedside, he pointed to the bag by the side of my bed. 'There's a few bits and pieces in the bag, a change of skiddies, socks and a couple of the local newspapers, which will make for some interesting reading – you and Jacko made the headlines and stirred up a hornets' nest. Right, I'm off,' said the boss. 'Oh, by the way, H, when you get out of hospital, I'm sending you to Liverpool for a few days' *R&R (rest and recuperation), help you get over this little episode. A couple of the lads will pick you up and drop you off at the ferry terminal. They will have your ferry tickets and some cash. Enjoy a few days with your new Scouse girlfriend, Nancy – nice name that – and when you get back we can get back to business.'

Then, with a broad smile, he turned and left. How the fuck did he know about my new girlfriend? I had told nobody on the unit. He even knew her fucking name. I must have been checked out more than I knew before they gave me this job. No wonder he knew Nancy's name, with a surname like O'Finnigan. He, the boss, had to know where Nancy and her family loyalties lay. They had only checked out her whole fucking family. What a unit. A unit that doesn't exist, with no name.

We knew on this unit that if we ever got taken by the IRA we would be classed as deserters from our relevant battalions or corps. No one wanted to know, or even admit, that this secretive unit ever existed. We would be nothing to do with the British army, we would be deserters, so our regiments would wash their hands of us. However, in the near future, after making a few more headlines, the army would eventually admit we did exist and, later still, they would eventually christen us and give us a name.

Reaching into the bag the boss had left for me, I pulled out a couple of local newspapers. Right across the front pages of both papers was a picture of our car smashed to bits against a telephone box and wall. My doctor was passing by my bed and he commented on the state of our car and said, 'I don't know how you got out of that alive with just a few bumps and bruises, someone must have been looking after you.'

'I reckon so, doc,' I said, as I read the headlines.

'Fury Over Spy Car Crash' read one headline; 'Special Air Service Death Squads' another one; 'Army Secret Civvy Squads' a third. No one knew who we were, so the press were putting their own moniker on us. One story read: 'The Northern Ireland Civil Rights Association will prepare evidence for the court of Human Rights in Strasbourg claiming to prove the existence of "British Army Murder Gangs operating in plain clothes". An army spokesman denied that the new unit is planned along the roles of the Special Air Service.' Another story read:-

> An army spokesman last night commented on the policy of sending soldiers out on the streets of Belfast in plain clothes. He said, 'We think it is necessary when we are put in the position of a virtual police force. We have got to operate as a quasi police force at times and like any police force we need detectives.' The spokesman added, 'If you put me in the corner on ethics, I would point out the ethics of the enemy. If we are going to have murderers and terrorists roaming our streets and towns trying to put us back to the dark ages, then we need to have people, well trained people, who are able to go out to find them. To play and beat them at their own murderous games.'
>
> These terrorists who use people, torture and kill

and maim need to be brought down by any means available to us. Details of how these squads operate is secret, but for obvious reasons they carry arms including submachine guns in case they have to fight their way out of a tight situation. They operate in a special unit, the name of which has not yet been security cleared for use outside the army. They work unattached to any regiment or unit serving in Ulster. They are a completely independent unit answering only to the few top people who set this unit up.'

A senior officer added last night, 'They are not in the business to make arrests, but they are specialists operating in very dangerous areas of greater risk than is experienced by the ordinary soldier in Belfast. That is not to say the ordinary soldiers are not well trained or brave. The world knows about the British soldiers. They are second to none,' he added.

I was lying in my bed taking in all the shit I've been reading, and inwardly fuming, when the jovial orderly appeared and handed me an official looking letter, 'from the Queen,' he said, laughing. On opening the letter, I found it to be from 'Major General HQ, N.I.' wishing me a quick recovery from my injuries (nice of him). After reading the papers over again, I came to the conclusion 'shit happens'.

Time to leave hospital. I said my goodbyes to the doctor and nurses who looked after me, and to the jovial orderly. Also to a couple of patients I'd chatted to over the last couple of days. Picking up my plastic bag with my few possessions I made my way to the exit of the military ward. The two armed guards wished me luck as they opened the door for me. I had long hair, a moustache and a couple of days' stubble on my chin. The guards had already made their minds up which regiment I was in. Rumours were always rife when they see a Brit soldier looking the way I did. These two guards wore the cap badge of the Royal Green Jackets. Bloody good soldiers with a fine reputation throughout the army.

Waiting outside the ward for me was my mate from the unit. 'Hi, H,' he greeted, reaching out his hand, which I shook.

'Hello Charlie, good to see you. Sad about Jacko.'

'It could have been worse,' he replied.

'How come?,' I said.

'It could have been me,' he said, with a wry grin.

Charlie didn't mean no harm by this comment. It was his way, just banter. In this unit we fiercely looked after each other. We trained hard and we fought hard and when we lose a friend, although it hurts bad, we use banter and crack jokes. It's our way of getting over the pain.

'Lets go,' Charlie said, 'Bill is waiting for us by the delivery entrance with the car. Taking the back way out of the hospital to keep away from the civvy wards. Best to be seen by as few civvies as possible.' On leaving the back entrance, I could see Bill, another close friend, and our car. Seeing us approaching, Bill jumped out of the car and opened the door for us. He shook my outstretched hand then threw his arms around me. Big hug.

He nearly broke my already bruised ribs. 'Glad to see you, glad to see you're not hurt,' he said. We all got into the car, Charlie riding shotgun and me in the back. Bill started up and we drove off, heading towards the ferry terminal. At our destination, Bill pulled over. 'Right, H, we've got you a suitcase with some of your shit in it. Should do you for a couple of days. Here's your ferry tickets and a few bob from the boss. The boss said have a good few days off with Nancy,' he said.

I grabbed my suitcase and said, 'I'll have a few beers for you two scrotes in Liverpool. See you, Charlie, see you, Bill, and thanks for everything. Thank the boss for me when you see him.

'See you, H,' they said in harmony. Turning, I boarded the ferry. This was an unexpected few days off and I hoped to make the most of them. I had already phoned Nancy to let her know I would be in Liverpool on the morning ferry. She had already asked me questions of why I was coming home so soon. She wasn't expecting me back. I had told her nothing about the last few days, just that I was owed a few days' R&R. Nancy didn't know much about the army until she met me. All her family were seafaring stock; she had family on the tug boats in the Mersey. Her brother was in the merchant navy and a couple of her uncles were in the Royal Navy. I was the first soldier she knew. I didn't tell her much about this tour in Belfast, only that I would be wearing civvies and not uniform. This seemed to please her because she thought if I was in civvies and not uniform I wouldn't be an easy target for some IRA sniper, that the IRA wouldn't know anything about me. I said nothing to make her feel differently, I just didn't want her to worry.

I made my way to the reception to get my cabin key. Getting to my room, I slipped the key card through the slot. On entering my room, bunk cabin, whatever the matelots call it, I threw my kit onto one of the beds, then turned to lock the door and headed for the bar. Two or three pints, then get my head down. I plonked myself on a stool at the bar and ordered a lager from the over friendly barman, 'Mm, nice, man!'

Getting my beer, I held it in both hands, resting it on the bar, just staring into the golden liquid, a tear forming in my eye, my mind in turmoil, thinking about Jacko. I had never met his wife or daughters, but he never shut up about them. He'd showed me pictures of his family, three lovely daughters and a beautiful wife. He was immensely proud of his family and now he was lying in a coma in the Royal Victoria Hospital, dying. Lifting my beer, I took a long gulp. 'To you, Jacko,' I soliloquised.[1] I had two more beers and went back to my bunk for a kip. Hopefully I would dream and get a little respite from my thoughts of Jacko and his family, and maybe dream of Nancy.

It was a calm crossing and I slept quite well. I dreamt of a beautiful green-eyed beauty waiting for me in Liverpool. Waking early, I went into my morning ritual. Shave, shit, shower, not always in that order. Finishing my ablutions, I went and grabbed some breakfast in one of the restaurants. The ship wasn't far off docking now, so I went and got my kit and made my way up to the deck ready to disembark. The ship started to slow right down, just gently cruising down the Mersey. What a beautiful sight the Liverpool skyline is. The ship finally berthed and, after what seemed an eternity, people began to disembark. I joined the flow of people to the terminal exit and as I left I could see Nancy standing next to her brother, Steven, who had obviously accompanied her to make sure she was okay. I waved and shouted her name. She saw me and ran to me, falling into my arms. I pulled her close and held her tight. I could feel her heart beating against my chest. I held her beautiful face in my hands and looked into those lovely green eyes that were starting to well up with tears. What a wonderful creature I had found. Then I kissed her.

Steven came over to us and put his arms around both of us. He said, 'Welcome home, H.' He then shook my hand with a firm handshake. He already treated me like a brother, and I knew his welcome home was genuine. Welcome home, yes, I thought, this will be my real home someday. I had never had what you could call a real home, a real family life, so those words from Steven made me feel, at long last, that I had found a home, a family and hopefully a wife in Nancy. This Scouse family treats me well, I thought. I am happy here.

The whole family went out for a meal on my first night home. The next couple of days Nancy and I went out with her brothers to clubs and pubs and we all had a great time. It was good to go to a club or a bar with little fear of getting shot, or your arse blown off. I admire the people of Northern Ireland. They go about their daily business, to work, theatres or clubs, trying to live as normal a life as possible. Not letting the terrorist scum win the day. One day, maybe the people of Northern Ireland will get the peace they pray for. I know lots of soldiers have died or been maimed fighting for their peace. I hope it's not been in vain.

*

My five days of R&R went by so swiftly and it was time to say my goodbyes (yet again) and return to my unit in Belfast. I said goodbye to Nancy's family, and Steven and Nancy accompanied me to the ferry. I shook Steven's hand and gave Nancy a hug, whispering in her ear, 'I love you'. I boarded the ship and made my way to the deck next to the dockside, so I could wave to Nancy and Steven. I put my hands on the rail of the ship, looking down at my Nancy. She was looking up at me, eyes starting to well up with tears. 'It won't be long, Nancy,' I shouted as the ship eventually started to pull away from the dock. She turned her back to me, shoulders shaking. I knew she was crying. She didn't want me to see how upset she was. Steven had his arm round her trying to console her. He raised his hand in a wave. I could see the sadness in his eyes. I waved back as the ship started to gather speed.

My own eyes welling up, I made my way to my cabin and laid down on one of the beds. I started to reminisce on when I first met Nancy. I was a physical training instructor in Park Hall Barracks, Oswestry. Nancy, first time away from home, worked in the NAAFI. I remember asking her where she was from, and when she said Liverpool, I thought, you can fuck off, they are all nutters from there. How wrong I was. Scousers are lovely people with a cutting sense of humour. They have got some lunatics, but so have all cities. Yes, I like Liverpool. I like the people and, god willing, one day with a lovely wife, I would settle there.

On the ferry back to Belfast, I had my meals, but no booze. Drinking on our unit was taboo. We had to have our wits about us one hundred per cent of the time. Booze slows your reaction time, and one day your reactions might save your life. The last few days in Liverpool, as good as they were, I have now got to get them out of my mind. I'm going back to my unit and the work we do is foremost.

It wouldn't be long before the ferry docked in Belfast, so I showered, got dressed and collected my gear together ready to disembark. After docking, I joined the flow of people leaving the ferry and, through the terminal, waiting for me, were Billy and Charlie with big grins on their faces.

'Well, did you have a good time?' Charlie said.

'Yeh alright, keep your dirty thoughts to yourselves,' I said, smiling.

We walked over to the nearby car park and got into our car. Bill started up and drove out of the terminal heading towards our base. We were driving through the countryside when Bill found a quiet layby and pulled the car over. Charlie, who was in the front seat, leaned over and handed me a 9mm Browning pistol saying, 'It's loaded, ten rounds and one up the spout and safety on.' I signed for it. He continued, 'Out of our armoury, so when we get to base you can re-sign for the pistol and ammo.'

'Thanks, mate,' I said. I felt a bit naked without a gun, giving the gun a once over. Bill pulled out of the layby saying, 'It won't be long before we get back to Newtownards and back to business.'

We drove up to the main gates of the military unit and Bill pulled our car into the searching bay and switched off the engine. The armed guards knew their stuff and gave us a good pretend search, patting us down giving no signs of surprise when they felt the 9mms tucked into our waist bands or shoulder holsters. Putting the mirrors under the car, searching the boot, pretending to look at our fake IDs. This all had to be done in case of any prying eyes. We had to be treated like any other civilian visitor to the camp. After the search, we got back into our car and drove to the far side of the camp, down a small lane, past a copse to where our unit was located. The double gates were already being opened by Rob as we approached. Bill drove through the open gate and parked the car, Rob shutting the gates behind us. We all got out of the car and went over to the unloading bay and, one by one, we made our weapons safe, each taking turns pointing the pistols at the sandbags and unloading. On unloading we showed each other the pistols were made safe. No round up the spout, no magazine on the weapon, working parts forward, trigger squeezed and safety catch on.

Rob said, 'There's some coffee and sandwiches in the telly room. Dinner is getting delivered from the cookhouse at 1800 hours and at 2000 hours, the boss is giving us a briefing, so you can stand down till then.' Rob then made his way back to the HQ hut. Rob let the chef know daily how many meals to deliver. It was not an ideal set up, but we were a new unit and there would be lots of teething problems, minor ones I hoped. It was all a new learning process, but we had been well trained to get on with it. It's not ideal that the guards, cooks and a few others know of us, but not what we do, but at least we are on the same side. Our training will hopefully bring us through the trials ahead. Our new unit is already putting lots of IRA men behind bars and sent some to meet their makers, and we hoped we would continue to do so.

Six of us were sitting around a couple of tables in our rest area, eating the dinner which had just been delivered and chatting. We knew roughly what the boss was going to talk to us about. The boss at the moment was debriefing two of our lads that had just finished a three-day op in the Whiterock area of Belfast. I was sure that when the boss had gleaned all the information out of them he would set up our next task. Finishing our meal, we still had an hour to go before the boss's briefing, so we sat down and watched the telly and generally relaxed. Outside, it had just started pissing down, the rain thrashing against the corrugated iron sheets like hailstones. Later Rob, who had only come about a hundred yards, opened the door to our hut and said, 'Come on, lads, time for the boss's O group.' Rob was dripping from head to foot. He looked like a drowned rat. In just a hundred yards, the rain had soaked him. Grabbing our coats, we rushed towards the briefing room.

On entering and shaking our coats dry, the boss said, 'Sit down, lads.' We hung our coats up and sat down facing the boss. Two of our lads were already seated next to the boss. 'Okay, lads,' the boss continued, 'Pat and Mick here next to me have just been on a three-day op in the Whiterock area of Belfast.'

Pat and Mick, I thought, you could not make it up.

The boss continued. 'They have just spent three days in a derelict, rat-infested, cockroach-ridden, flea house.' A murmur of laughter rippled through the room. 'When they finished their op, Pat and Mick had to be deloused along with the driver of the extraction car in the RVH, and the car had a bloody good spraying and the spanner assures me the car is fit to be driven again.' More laughter. 'Anyway, lads, you all know about the carjackings that have been going on! Well, Pat and Mick got some good information and got some good photographs of two of the culprits. The photo reels I've given to the local intelligence officer to get developed by the battalion's photographer. He assures me the photographs will be ready first thing tomorrow morning.'

Over the three-day op, the two IRA men stopped

umpteen cars but only hijacked three. Of most of the cars stopped, the IRA men seemed to know the occupants, smiling and talking to them and occasionally shaking hands. The first car that got hi-jacked was driven by a young lad, about twenty years of age. He got dragged out of his car with two pistols pointing at him. One of the IRA men clipped him round his head, at the same time pointing towards the Falls Road, the direction the young lad had driven from. The driver was then seen running away from the IRA men. The two IRA men then got into the car and drove down to the Donegall Road, turning right which would also lead to the Falls Road. They were only gone about fifteen minutes before the op saw them walking back up the road, where they resumed their place on the corner of the street.

'This tells me,' continued the boss, 'that there is a third party involved, getting rid of the hijacked cars. The second car they took was driven also by a young man with a girl passenger with two pistols pointing at them. They seemed to do exactly what they were told. The couple got out of the car and they both ran in the direction the IRA men pointed, the young girl in tears with the young man's arm round her shoulder. As like the first car, they drove off in it, returned back to their post fifteen minutes later. The third and last hijacking the op saw was the most brutal. After stopping the car, an IRA man was seen arguing with the occupants. The IRA man opened the driver's door, dragging an elderly man out and pistol-whipped him to the floor. The other occupant, an elderly lady, got out of the car and went to the old man's aid. She was crying and helped the old man to his feet. He had blood running down the side of his head. The IRA man grabbed him by the throat and shook him, he then pointed up the road with his pistol. The old couple were then seen to make their way back in the direction they had come. The cars that get taken get used for all kinds of things. They get burned out to block streets leading into their areas, get used in robberies or sold on, the proceeds going into the IRA's coffers.'

'On the desk in front of you,' the boss continued, 'is a map of the Westrock area, and I've marked off the street junction where these two scumbags have been operating from. On the corner of the junction is a house surrounded by a six- or seven-foot hedge. There's a gateway leading towards the house. The IRA men have been observed going through this gate and returning after a couple of minutes. The op assumed they were going for a piss against the hedgerow or they had access to a toilet in the house. It was a good junction and they chose it carefully. If a military foot or vehicle patrol came towards them in any direction, they would have plenty of time to escape. They, I'm sure, would have a pre-planned escape route, starting through the gate in the hedge and over a few back gardens hiding their pistols on the way. Over the three days, they were observed between two and three o'clock and stayed till between five and six o'clock. They appeared for the full three days, so there's no reason why they won't be there tomorrow. Well, I'm hoping they will be there and we get a good result.'

The boss continued, 'I'm going to study all this intelligence I've got and come up with a plan of action, which will be happening tomorrow. I've already decided to have two cars ready, but don't know yet if both crews will get used. The first car will be you, H, as the commander. Bill will be your driver and Charlie the machine gunner. Your call sign will be "ALPHA ONE". Got that, H?'

'Yes, boss,' I said.

'The second car will be Jock, the commander, Will your driver and Rod machine gunner. Your call sign will be "ALPHA TWO", base being Alpha. Got that, Jock?'

'Yes, boss,' Jock said.

'Right, lads, I'll have a plan sorted out tonight and I want you all to be back here by 1000 hours tomorrow morning when I should have the photographs back as well. Get a good night's rest, lads. Goodnight.'

'Goodnight,' we all said in unison.

The following morning we were all up early and after breakfast we spent almost an hour preparing our weapons. Charlie had his submachine gun in pieces, checking all the working parts. His gun had a suppressor (silencer) on it. I stuck to my 9mm Browning, as did Bill. As I was cleaning my 9mm, Rob came in the room carrying a folder. 'Sign here, H,' he said.

'What's it for?' I said.

'For your 9mm and ammunition, keeps everything above board.'

'Okay, mate, no problems,' I said, signing the forms.

The spanner came into the rest area and told us only Alpha One would be needed on the brief at 1000 hours, but Alpha Two could sit in and listen if they wanted to. 'Okay, spanner,' said Jock, 'Alpha two will sit in for the brief, it will keep us in the picture.' Five minutes to ten found us all entering the briefing room. Alpha One sat up near the front and Alpha Two sat behind us.

Entering the room, the boss said, 'Relax and listen, boys.' The boss started the brief about the orders for opening fire in Northern Ireland, the yellow card, as it was called. 'Right, lads, you all know the yellow card. You also know how many soldiers have been killed trying to carry these orders out. See guys carrying guns and you tell them to halt, drop their weapons and put their hands up and, in those few seconds you lose the advantage and could end up dead. I'm not telling you to be murderers, but we work in different circumstances than a uniformed soldier, so I'm telling you if in doubt, take them out. Do you all understand?'

'Yes, boss,' we all said in unison.

The boss handed us photographs of the two IRA men who had been doing the carjackings, saying, 'The intelligence officer delivered these earlier. Take a good look at them, lads. You will know one of them straight away. The army's been after him for almost a year now, and we know he's wanted for at least two sectarian murders. The other one is not on our radar, a new face to us. Pat and Mick done a fucking good job getting all this information. Now we are going to act on it. Right, Alpha One, I've decided to use one car only.' The boss had a large-scale map on the wall behind him of the area we would be operating in. He pointed to a junction on the map, saying, 'This is where the two IRA men have been up to mischief. You should have highlighted it on your own maps. I will go over what your operation is going to be. I know you all know the area well, but I want it fixed firmly in your heads.' The boss pointed a stick at the map behind him, tracing the route as he told us, 'You will travel down the Falls Road, turning left into Salle Road, drive to the end of this road and turn right into St John's Square and Donegall Road. This is the junction where they should be. Drive slowly past them. If they don't react, do nothing, just carry on driving. If they look as though they are reaching for a weapon, take them out. Bill, you have your wits about you. If there is any shooting, they will be out of their houses like a swarm of flies. Don't hang around, drive straight up the Donegall Road, back to the Falls Road, turn right and get lost in the traffic. The Falls Road is a busy road, so you should have no trouble mingling. Less than ten minutes away a military mobile unit will be on standby on the Whiterock Road should you need aid in any way. You know what the the IRA men look like now, having studied their mugshots. I am in direct contact with the army unit, so I will let them know if the shit hits the fan. You will be in contact with the sparky at all times during the op – keeping us updated at all times is essential. You will leave here at 1300 hours. It should take forty minutes to get there, so the IRA men should already be there. Any questions?'

'Everything seems clear, boss,' I said.

'Right, finish off getting ready, re-check all your gear, and good luck.'

We left the briefing room and went back to our rest area. We re-checked our weapons and ammunition. We were all in scruff order as though we had been working on a building site. All of us wore donkey jackets, which helped us to blend in and also helped to conceal our weapons.

The spanner came over to us and he handed Bill a set of car keys saying our car for the day was the dark blue Vauxhall Viva. 'Sparky has checked the communications and everything is fine. I've checked the car over,' continued the spanner, 'and she is running like a Rolls,' he said, smiling. Bill had already driven all our cars as he was recognised as being our best driver.

We made our way to the loading and unloading bay

and armed our weapons, then the four of us went over to our car where Bill gave it the once-over himself. Charlie got into the back seat, cocking his machine gun and putting the safety catch on. This done, he concealed it under a towel on the seat next to him. Bill got behind the wheel and I got in the front passenger seat. The spanner closed my door and headed towards the double gates, where all the boys that weren't on duty and the boss had gathered. While the spanner was opening the gates, Bill started our car up and headed towards the exit. Bill and I also cocked our weapons, one up the spout and the safety catch on. On leaving our compound, all the lads were laughing and joking, generally taking the piss and wishing us good luck. The last words I heard on leaving were the boss saying, 'If in doubt, take them out and get back safe.'

Bill drove the car down the Sydenham Bypass towards Belfast. Charlie, looking out the side window, said it looked like it was going to piss down. 'If it does, it will fuck everything up. I can't see those IRA men standing on a corner of the road while it's pissing down.'

'With a little luck, it will hold off,' said Bill.

Bill, turning into Divis, Street said, 'Not far to go now, lads. We'll soon be on the Falls Road and it looks like the rain is going to hold.' Bill swung the car left into Salle Road. 'We should be spotting the IRA men soon.' There weren't many cars around, which wasn't such a bad thing. The IRA men had chosen their spot carefully, for they could see the length of all the roads from their vantage point. If a military foot patrol or Land Rover patrol approached them, they would have plenty of time to jump over a few back gardens, hiding their pistols on the way, and escape.

'There they are,' said Bill.

'Okay, Charlie, get that machine gun ready and, Bill, you know the score. Drive slowly past them and if there's any shooting, put your foot down and get us out of dodge.'

As we neared the IRA men, one of them stepped into the road, holding his hand up to flag us down. He wasn't holding a weapon, and neither was his mate.

'Okay, Bill, don't stop. Pull out and drive slowly round him.'

As we passed them, I turned round, kneeling on my seat, pistol in my hand, but still out of sight, with the safety catch off. Looking out of the car's back window, Charlie was already kneeling on the back seat with his SMG at the ready. Charlie was to the left of the seat so I could see everything that was going on to his right. The second IRA man stepped into the street next to his mate, and both of them started to reach under their coats. One of them was fucking fast – he had his pistol in the aiming position in a split second. I don't know who fired first, it happened so damn fast. Pistol shots and a long burst of machine gun fire mixed with my three shots being fired through the shattered rear window. In those split seconds, I saw both the IRA men falling to the ground, pistols spilling out of their hands. Bill had already put his foot down, so I knew he hadn't been hit.

'You okay, Charlie?' I said.

'Yes, mate, fuck me, that was close.'

Bill was just turning into the flow of traffic on the Falls Road when the heavens opened. The rain came down in torrents, drowning poor Charlie on the back seat. Only seconds had lapsed since the shooting.

'Okay, lads, I'm giving base a sit-rep. Hello, Alpha,

this is Alpha One, over, send over, Alpha One contact this call sign, no casualties, two down, over. Alpha, roger out.'

'What do you mean, H, no casualties this call sign?' Charlie whinged.

'We are all okay, aren't we?' I said.

'I'm like a drowned rat in the back here.'

Bill and I had a little laugh at Charlie's misfortune.

I was putting the safety catch on my weapon and looked at my hands – they were trembling and my heart was thumping away. Fucking hell, I thought, this has affected me more than I thought it would. Charlie had already put his safety on and concealed his gun once more under his now soaking wet towel.

It wasn't long before we were pulling into our base, getting a few weird looks off the guards who had been instructed to wave us through. Bill drove on to our unit where the spanner was waiting to open the gates. Driving through the double gates, the spanner said, 'What the fuck have you done to my car?' Grinning, he continued, 'You all look like shite.'

Bill parked the car and the three of us went over to the unloading bay to make our weapons safe. 'When you have unloaded, put your weapons away and report to the boss in the briefing room,' said the spanner.

'Okay, spanner, no probs,' I said.

Entering the briefing room, the boss was already waiting for us, and sparky was manning the radio. 'Sit down, lads,' said the boss. 'What happened, H?'

I told the boss exactly how it went down, omitting nothing. I said, 'Charlie saw a little more than I did.'

The boss said, 'What did you see, Charlie?'

'As I was looking out the back window, the IRA man

on the pavement stepped onto the road next to his mate. Then they both reached under their jackets and both started to raise their pistols. I let loose with a burst of my SMG. Like H said, boss, it was all over in a few seconds.'

'Okay, lads. Thanks, Charlie. As soon as you let me know two IRA men were down,' the boss continued, 'I got onto the intelligence officer of the resident battalion. I asked him to keep an eye on the hospitals and also to put an op on the doctor's surgery, just in case. The boss continued, 'It's a waiting game now, lads, so go and sort your weapons out and get something to eat and we will have a chat later.'

Just as we were leaving the office, the spanner came in and said to the boss, 'The car was hit three times, boss.'

'Bloody hell, let's go and have a shufti (look),' said the boss.

We all stood round the car while the spanner showed us the bullet scars. One had hit low down in the boot and one had grazed the roof of the car. The spanner left the best till last. One round had entered through the shattered back window, passed through the top right of the front passenger seat and embedded itself into the console. 'How the fuck did that miss me – miss us?' That was closer than I thought. Well, I reckon it just wasn't our time.

We made our way to the rest room. It was still pissing down. We cleaned our weapons, showered and got into our trackies and just tried to relax a little. We were all in our own little worlds. I don't know how Charlie felt; he was curled up on one of the easy chairs, eyes closed. The burst of fire he put down was fourteen rounds.

It was 2030 hours when the boss sent for us. We walked into the briefing room. All the other lads were already sat down. 'Okay, lads,' the boss said with a big grin on his face. I assumed he had good news for us. We all sat down facing the boss when he started, 'I've got lots of information off the army lads and their intelligence officer. I've been told one of the IRA men ended up in the morgue of the RVH, he'd been hit six times. The op that the intelligence officer put on the doctor's surgery really paid off. The op reported that a car pulled up at the doctor's and two men got out and carried a person into the surgery. With this information, the army sent in a snatch squad. A platoon of squaddies raided the surgery and found the doctor operating on a badly wounded man. The two men who took him in surrendered right away and they were armed. I guess they didn't want to end up like their mate. The snatch squad had their own ambulance, doctor and medics. They put the injured IRA man in the ambulance and took him under escort to the RVH. I've been told he's in a bad way. The driver of the car was also arrested for questioning. He was unarmed.'

'I've left the best till last,' said the boss. 'When the squaddies arrested the doctor they also searched the surgery. Behind a large wardrobe, they found what can only be described as a broom cupboard. In this cupboard were four American ArmaLite rifles, seven assorted pistols, six hand grenades, one submachnine gun, hundreds of rounds of ammunition, fourteen detonators and bomb-making kits, also books on how to assemble bombs.'

Fuck me, I thought, he rattled off that lot without a breath. What a memory.

'The squaddies also found out the good doctor was also a surgeon and the IRA's quartermaster. It looks like he will be sent down for a very long time. So to re-cap,' said the boss, 'one IRA man dead, one fighting for his life, one IRA surgeon and quartermaster along with the three IRA men out the car, arrested. An arsenal of weapons and bombs that the IRA won't be killing people with, taken off the streets.'

An eruption of applause and cheers went up from all the lads in the room.

'Okay,' continued the boss, 'the commanding officer and his intelligence officer of the resident battalion both congratulated us for our intelligence. They heaped praises on us and said well done, that none of this could have been achieved without our help. Fucking well done, lads,' All of us started cheering and clapping again. Bloody hell, I thought, this unit is really pissing the IRA off.

We all started to disperse to our relevant room or the rest room with the boss's congratulations ringing in our ears.

Springfield Road

The following day I was called into the the boss's office, he was sitting behind his desk as I entered. 'Grab a seat H'.

'Thanks boss'.

'Listen H, several months ago an army footpatrol arrested an IRA man, a deserter from the British army. He has been in the IRA for a couple of years and we knew he was up to all kinds of shit, anyway, after a good grilling and the threat of putting him away for twenty years or so he agreed to turn informant for army intelligence'.

Over the last seven months he has given us some real good intel, and we have made quite a few arrests and stopped a couple of sectarian murders. His name is Jake Quin, a couple of week's ago he handed himself into army custody at Springfield Road police station, he informed his "Handler" that he wants to return to the UK because he thinks he has been compromised by the IRA, we've agreed to escort him back but he must serve six months in military nick before he gets discharged from the army. He's agreed to these terms, 'I don't.' Nobody trusts the slimy git, we think he is up to something'.

'You H will be escorting him back to the UK, so for the next week you will be attached to the RUC at Springfield Road police station. Over the week it will be your job to befriend him and gain his confidence, then you will escort him back to Liverpool. As far as he is concerned you are taking him back to nick but he doesn't know which one. However, when you get to Liverpool you will give him the opportunity to escape. As soon as you get on the ferry MI5 will be putting a tail on you, then when he does a runner MI5 will follow him to his cronies or safe house. Surveillance OPS can be put on him and whoever he leads the MI5 people to'

'That's it H, pack what kit you think you might need, Charlie and Bill have been told to take you to Springfield Road.'

'Ok boss I'll get on with it'.

An hour later saw me entering past the army checkpoint into Springfield Road police station where I was introduced to an army sergeant. 'You must be H', he said and outstretched his hand which I shook. 'I'm Bryan mate and I've been put in charge of the slimy shit, I tell you just being in his company makes you cringe, I would love to throttle him, a fuckin British soldier joining the IRA, anyway H, I'll show you where your room is. The scrotes in the last cell on the left, when you want to see him the OPS desk people will let you into his cell. Your boss informed me you were coming and what he wants you to do. Good luck with that mate'.

After I'd sorted my room out I went to introduce myself to 'Jake'. An army full corporal who was on duty at the OPS desk, he let me into his cell, then closed the door behind me. I looked across to this horrible evil looking git lying on his bunk; I put a forced smile on my face and extended my hand, saying, 'Hi Jake, my names H and I will be escorting you back to England next week'.

He got up out of his bunk and shook my hand, a clammy cold weak handshake, Brian was right, just looking at him made you want to throttle him.

'Jake, how come you ended up in a police cell in Northern Ireland' (as if I didn't know). We both sat down on his bed, he started giving me the story of his family being of Irish decent and he was pissed off about the way the 'Brits', his words not mine, treated the Irish. He could see nothing wrong with the IRA, they were a legal army fighting for Irish freedom as far as he was concerned. I almost blurted out, 'what about the scum IRA torture squads', but thought better of it. I was cringing listening to the bile that he was speaking and pretending that he had a few good points.

For the next week I took his food daily, supplied him with ciggies and generally gained his trust, after a week of listening to his crap everything was set for me to take him back to England. I'd already been briefed, I had ferry tickets to Liverpool, though I wouldn't be able to see Nancy this trip as I was armed. I had train tickets to Birmingham, changing at Crewe with a bit of luck the scrote will do a runner before we get to Birmingham.

We arrived in Liverpool on a freezing cold morning. I tried to spot whoever was trailing us but to no avail, having only had months of training for this, they had years. I told Jake we would jump into a taxi to the station where we would get something to eat.

Arriving at Lime Street Station I paid the taxi and we both entered the station. 'Come on Jake, there's a cafe over there'.

We sat down next to the door, a convenient place to sit should Jake decide to do a runner. 'Look Jake,' I said, 'don't do a runner. It took me a long time to get my tapes, if I lose you before I get you to nick they will bust me'.

'No problem H, you've been good to me, I won't do a bunk.'

We got a sandwich and coffee each, we chatted away and I said, 'I'm going to the bogs Jake, I need a crap.' I opened the door and entered the bog, almost closing the door behind me, I left a slight opening where I could just about see Jake.

He stood up and moved his head from left to right, scanning all around him, this is it I thought, 'the bastards going to do a runner, go ahead you evil little twat, take the bait', but to my disappointment he sat back down again. I waited a couple more minutes and returned to our table.

'Thanks Jake,'

'For what,'

'For not doing a runner,' I said.

'Told you H, I just want this over with, serve my time and get on with my life'.

Fuck me, I thought, he's not going to do a runner. He sounded so sincere.

We got on the train heading for Crewe, it wasn't a long journey, we just chatted away, with him doing most of the talking, mainly about his hate for the British Army. I really wanted to chop him in the throat to shut him up. We arrived at Crewe and had fourty minutes before the Birmingham train left, I was still trying to spot who was following us but they were good, I saw nothing suspicious.

There was a train about to leave on the other side of the platform. I thought, here goes. 'Jake, I'm just going to get some food and drink for our journey, I'll only be five minutes.'

I entered the cafe and lost myself behind an advertising screen, I peeked round the side of the screen and watched as Jake got on the train that was about to leave, looking down the length of the platform I still couldn't suss out who was following us.

Then Jake got off to the train, 'What the fuck's he doing,' he walked to the next carriage and got back on the train, walked the length of the carriage and got back off, this was like something out of Laurel and Hardy. Just as the train was pulling away he jumped back on. 'Yes, fuckin yes, result'.

Now all I had to do was get back to my unit. Pitty I couldn't pop in to see Nancy, our time would come.

Arriving back at my unit my boss said, 'Well done H, we'll get the info in a few days time off the intel officer, We will soon know what the bastards up to.'

'Thanks Boss', I said, heading for my bunk and a good nights rest.

The following morning Charlie and I got called in to see the boss. 'Hi lads', he greeted.

'Hi boss', we said in unison.

Your Battalion H, is due to finish their tour in two weeks' time, and your time with us will be over. You, Charlie, will be heading back to your unit in a few days, earlier than H. From now until you leave, I won't be sending you out on any more ops. I don't want anything happening to you. I will be sending you both home to your families in one piece. So, for the next week or so you can help around the base. You can work with the spanner or with sparky on the radios, or give a hand in the armoury if you want, lads, just keep yourselves occupied. Once again, thank you both for your good work and professionalism. It's been my privilege to have you on my team. That's it for now, lads, go and relax, watch the telly or something.'

'Thanks, boss,' we both said as we left the room.

Charlie said he was going for a lie down, and I told him I was going to relax in the rest room. I entered our rest area and plonked myself into an easy chair, grabbing an old newspaper off the top of the book shelf.

Jock, who was the only one in the room besides me, greeted me as I sat down saying, 'Most of the lads are out tonight on various ops.' I told Jock the boss had stopped me and Charlie from going out anymore, because we hadn't got long left before we finished our time here. 'Yeh,' replied Jock, 'that's the way the boss works.'

I looked at the headlines of the newspaper I had picked up. It read, 'Soldier in Civvies Shoots Dead a Post Office Raider.' I read the article and said to Jock. 'The newspapers never give it to you straight, do you know what happened here?' I asked, showing Jock the headlines.

'Didn't Charlie tell you the story, H?'

'No, why? What happened?' I said.

Jock started the story: a couple of the lads were stopping at a village post office about seven miles from here to buy some stamps and post a few letters. It was Charlie and Bill who were driving. Anyway, Bill pulled up on the opposite side of the road to the post office. Charlie got out the car, Bill staying behind the wheel. Charlie noticed a guy on a motorbike right outside the post office, with the bike's engine running; the guy on the bike kept looking over his shoulder towards the post office. As Charlie crossed the road two shots rang out from inside the post office, and this guy came running out with a pistol in one hand and a rucksack in the other.

The gunman put two more shots into the post office as he ran towards the guy on the motor bike. Charlie, who already had his pistol in the aiming position after hearing the first two shots, screamed at the gunman to drop his weapon. The gunman had started to turn towards Charlie with his pistol raised when Charlie gave him a double tap to the chest. The gunman dropped to the gutter, his gun spilling out of his hand, along with the rucksack. The guy on the motorbike didn't hang round – he sped off down the road, leaving his mate behind. Charlie went over to the gunman and checked him out. Not many people would survive a double tap to the chest, and this gunman was one of them.

A woman came out of the post office, crying. Charlie asked her if anyone was hurt. Although hysterical, she managed to say that no one else was hurt and that she was the postmistress. Charlie grabbed the gunman's pistol and handed the rucksack to the postmistress. Then, turning, Charlie ran back to the car and Bill, who already had the engine running, headed back to base.

'Fuck me, Jock. How did the papers know it was a soldier in civvies that killed the gunman?'

'When Bill and Charlie got back to base they were debriefed by the boss. The boss then told our intelligence officer and the local police. I assume it was the police who informed the media.'

'Bloody hell, Jock. Bill and Charlie never said a word to me.' I said.

'Modest bastards, aren't they!' said Jock.

It was 2330 hours when I said goodnight to Jock and headed for my room. I was just lying on my bed, thoughts running amok. If it had been pissing down, those two IRA men wouldn't have got shot. Not that day anyway. The doctor along with the three IRA men wouldn't have been arrested, and that arms cache wouldn't have been found. I thought of the IRA men Charlie and I had shot. It's not a good feeling taking a person's life; they were only in their teens. Life is precious, and those IRA men had families. Shit, what's the matter with me? Why am I thinking like this? They chose to go on the path of terrorism and they can't be left to run amok, killing, maiming, bombing and such. This last thought made me feel a little better. I closed my eyes and slept.

The next two weeks flew by. Charlie and I helped to man the radios with sparks and gave the spanner a hand cleaning his cars. We also helped in the armoury, cleaning the weapons. Charlie left the unit two days before me. He handed in his 9mm Browning and ammunition. He said his goodbyes to the lads and got into the rear seat of the car that was taking him to the ferry. Bill was driving, and Jock was the commander. All the lads that weren't out on operations gathered at the gates to wave their goodbyes. Bill drove up to the open gates and stopped so the boss could shake Charlie's hand. I saw a puzzled look on Charlie's face as he shook the boss's hand. The boss just smiled at Charlie and told Bill to drive on. I'd already said my emotional goodbyes to Charlie.

Two days to go for me now. I'd phoned Nancy and let her know I would be returning to my battalion in Tidworth and that I would be seeing her soon. I wrote a couple of letters to my family and generally got my kit ready for the off, back to sunny Tidworth.

My time came to be taken to the ferry terminal; I was going back on the evening ferry docking at Liverpool, so I was hoping I'd get a couple of hours with Nancy before

I continued my journey to Tidworth. Bill was my driver and Jock was the commander of our car.

Now it was my time to be waved off at the gate. I'd already handed in my 9mm pistol and ammunition. Bill pulled out the parking bay and headed for the gate. Bill stopped the car as he had done for Charlie, so the boss could shake my hand and, in that hand shake, I felt something passing from his hand to mine. He held his hand firmly with mine. He said, 'You know that story you told me about "the poison dwarf" giving you shit about your hair cut? Well, it looks like he will be getting you when you get back.'

'Don't worry, boss, I won't be giving him the pleasure. I will have a skinhead the next time he sees me.'

The boss looked me right in the eye and said, 'Thank you, H.' He turned and walked back towards the briefing room.

Spanner gave me a smile and a wave as he closed the gates behind us.

I opened my hand to see what the boss had slipped into it. No wonder Charlie looked puzzled if the boss gave him the same as what I had in my hand. It was a 'winged dagger' cap badge. I felt a lump in my throat and, yes, tears came into my eyes and rolled down my cheeks.

'Stop your blubbering, you soft shite,' said Bill, smiling as he drove me to the ferry terminal.

Ho yeh!! The powers to be finally gave our unit a name. It was the early days of the MRF.

The Military Reaction Force.

THE END.

Thank you for reading my book. I hope you enjoyed it.

H

Some dates, times and street names have been altered.

Notes

Glossary

7.62 – a calibre of round
CO – commanding officer, the officer in charge of a unit.
double tap – two rounds fired quickly at the same target, giving the maximum amount of damage
hogging irons – knife, fork and spoon
kit check – puke
MO – medical officer
MT yard – military transport yard
NAAFI – standing for the Navy, Army and Air Force Institutes, this refers to recreational buildings within barracks, providing recreational establishments, shops and services to servicemen and their families.
NCO – non-commissioned officer, i.e. corporals and lance corporals.
op – OP, observation post
pads – married personnel
PT Kit – physical training kit
R.P. – Regimental Police
Rupert – officer
RV – rendez-vous, an appointed place for troops or a fleet to assemble.
SMG – submachine gun
R&R – Rest and Recuperation
RMP – Royal Military Police
RSM – regimental sergeant major (razz man)
RVH – Royal Victorian Hospital

SLR – self-loading rifle
UDA – Ulster Defence Association

Endnotes

1. Jacko died of his injuries five months after going into a coma.
2. The 9mm Browning pistol stolen off me on the Newtownards Road went on to be the tool of several sectarian murders.
3. The IRA man 'Jake Quin' who absconded at Crew Railway Station was found two weeks later on a building site in Belfast. His kneecaps had been drilled through and most of his fingers were missing, those left had the finger nails removed.

    The bullet hole between his eyes I assume ended his misery.

www.ingramcontent.com/pod-product-compliance
Lightning Source LLC
Chambersburg PA
CBHW022358040426
42450CB00005B/246